GRAND STREET

New York

51

Front cover: Louise Lawler, *To Scale (Stella at Saatchi Headquarters, New York)*, detail, 1991–92

Back cover: David Hammons, *Blizzard Ball Sale*, 1983

"The Black Book" is adapted from *The Black Book* by Orhan Pamuk, to be published by Farrar, Straus & Giroux in January 1995. Translation copyright © 1994 by Guneli Gun. All rights reserved.

"New York and Me" copyright © 1994 by Alexander Cockburn.

"The Tunnel" copyright © 1994 by Margaret Morton.

Photograph (p. 73) copyright © E. Erwitt/Magnum Photos, Inc. and Nouvelles Images, SA.

Photographs (pp. 49–56) copyright © Louis Faurer.

Drawing by Roz Chast (p. 84) copyright © 1985 by The New Yorker Magazine, Inc.

Grand Street is set in ITC New Baskerville by Crystal Graphics, Houston, Tex., and printed by Wetmore and Company, Houston, Tex. Color separations and halftones are by Typografiks, Inc., Houston, Tex.

Grand Street (ISBN 1-885490-02-X) is published quarterly by Grand Street Press (a project of the New York Foundation for the Arts, Inc., a not-for-profit corporation), 131 Varick Street, #906, New York, N.Y. 10013. Contributions and gifts to Grand Street Press are tax-deductible to the extent allowed by law. This publication is made possible, in part, by a grant from the National Endowment for the Arts.

Volume Thirteen, Number Three (*Grand Street* 51–Winter 1995). Copyright © 1994 by New York Foundation for the Arts, Inc., Grand Street Press. All rights reserved. Reproduction, whether in whole or in part, without permission is strictly prohibited.

Second-class postage paid at New York, N.Y., and additional mailing offices. Postmaster: Please send address changes to *Grand Street* Subscription Service, Dept. GRS, P.O. Box 3000, Denville, N.J. 07834.

Subscription orders and address changes should be addressed to *Grand Street* Subscription Service, Dept. GRS, P.O. Box 3000, Denville, N.J. 07834. Subscriptions are $30 a year (four issues). Foreign subscriptions (including Canada) are $50 a year, payable in U.S. funds. Single-copy price is $10 ($12.99 in Canada). For subscription inquiries, please call (800) 807-6548.

Grand Street is distributed to the trade by D.A.P./Distributed Art Publishers, 636 Broadway, 12th floor, New York, N.Y. 10012, Tel: (212) 473-5119, Fax: (212) 673-2887, and to newsstands only by B. DeBoer, Inc., 113 E. Centre St., Nutley, N.J. 07110 and Fine Print Distributors, 6448 Highway 290 E., Austin, Tex. 78723. *Grand Street* is distributed in Australia and New Zealand by Peribo Pty, Ltd., 58 Beaumont Road, Mount Kuring-Gai, NSW 2080, Tel: (2) 457-0011.

GRAND STREET

Editor

Jean Stein

Managing Editor

Deborah Treisman

Art Editor

Walter Hopps

Assistant Editor

Howard Halle

Designer

Don Quaintance

Editorial Assistant

Julie A. Tate

Production Assistant

Elizabeth Frizzell

Interns

Jeffrey Rotter

Elisa Frohlich

Administrative Assistant

Lisa Brodus

Contributing Editors

Hilton Als, Anne Doran, Morgan Entrekin, Gary Fisketjon,
Raymond Foye, Jonathan Galassi, Barbara Heizer, Dennis Hopper,
Andrew Kopkind (1935–1994),
Jane Kramer, Olivier Nora, Erik Rieselbach, Edward W. Said,
Robert Scheer, Elisabeth Sifton, Jean Strouse, Jeremy Treglown,
Katrina vanden Heuvel, Gillian Walker, Drenka Willen

Publishers

Jean Stein & Torsten Wiesel

CONTENTS

*This issue is dedicated to the memory of
Andrew Kopkind (1935–1994).*

Pages from the Atlas: New York

Opening the Book
(Grand Central Station, New York City, U.S.A., 1991)
Scissoring legs and shadows scudding like clouds across the marble
proved to be destiny in action, for the people who rushed through
this concourse came from the rim of everywhere to be ejaculated
everywhere, redistributing themselves without reference to each
other. They were all about changing places. A few, like the small
girl who sat on the stairs holding her bald baby doll, or the lady
who stopped, shifted the strap of her handbag, and gazed at the
departure times for the New Haven Line, delayed judgment (and
an executive paused in his descent of the steps, snorted at the girl's
doll, and said: I thought that baby was real!) But no one *stayed*
here, except the souls without homes. Above the information
kiosk, the hands of the illuminated clock circled all the directions,
tranquilly, while the stone-muffled murmurs of the multitude rose
and condensed into meaningless animal sounds. There was a circle, and its spokes were their trajectories. But the circle turned!
They did not understand the strangeness of that. Creased black
trousers, naked brown legs, merciless knees, skirts and jeans, overalls swollen tight with floating testicles, paisley handbags passing
as smoothly as magic carpets. These made noise, had substance,
but the place became more and more empty as I sat there, because
none of it was *for* anything but itself. The belt of brass flowers that

crossed the ceiling's belly meant something, made the place more like a church: the sunken tunnels where the trains stretched themselves out, gleaming their lights, were the catacombs. One of those passageways went to the Montrealer, my favorite train. Canada's railroads continued north from Montreal, which was why when I peered into that tunnel (I'd ridden the Montrealer so many times, and wouldn't anymore), it was almost as if I could see all the way to Hudson Bay; one Canadian National sleeper did still go to Churchill—

A policeman came and told me to move on. So I went past the double green globes; I left the people who were going somewhere (a girl in high heels galloped by me, biting her lip with concentration, and one of her breasts struck my cheek); and I too went my way, obeying the same law that dispersed the others....

From **Cowbells**
(New York City and State, 1992)

So we know about ivy and trees, but what if the ivy were mere wires; what if the trees were only square white pillars in the dimness between trains; what if the leaves were incandescent lights? Then the forest would be light-spangled darkness, lit the way my legs glowed luminous green under a certain bar. Then I'd know I was in New York. Outside of this forest other trees whose wiry roots dangled down like ivy over the concrete wall of the parking lot. The Hudson River was a root boring past the chilly eastern towns whose wall-bricks were a patchwork of dirty colors. I'd thought I was going to go outside the city often but then I didn't because whenever I started planning to I got a bad feeling about it—usually after I remembered those dying trees.

Instead I visited the dog poisoner. He was not an evil man at all; he had rules. The dog had to have annoyed him more than once. Other people needed to have treated him badly at the same time. There could be no risk to him. Those conditions being met, he would lay down the strychnined meat. The dog would bolt that food, crunching bones between yellow teeth. The poison was in the best parts, the fatty parts. First the dog would stretch out, happily gnawing the last thick bone. Then suddenly it would cock its head. It raised its ears, listening alertly to the bells which only it could hear. Something was happening or had just begun to happen which the dog did not understand yet because the growling whimpering convulsions had not begun. The dog knew only that what was happening was extremely important. It chewed no bone; clanged the bronze bells of death.

Charity
(New York City, 1990)

You get on the bus and sit down because there are empty seats. A few minutes later, however, the aisle is a battlefield of sweet soft arms of women, of women's hands touching poles.

You give your seat to a woman with a baby.

A young girl across from you smiles at you. She too rises, and gives her seat to an old lady.

Presently the bus is emptier again. Only you and she are standing.

A seat appears beside you. You take it.

Now only the girl is standing. You look at her. She is as able to stand as you. She is carrying a heavy bag. You have a heavy pack. Should you offer her your seat?

You smile and do this.

She smiles and shakes her head.

You and she are very aware of each other. You and she feel sweetly about each other.

The bus pauses and she gets off; the bus pauses, and you get off. Already you have forgotten her face. But you remember her as the partner of this complex and unknown thing which was at its best blossoming when you and she could barely see each other through the jungle of arms and legs, hair and glasses and ringed fingers; you remember her sandaled foot, which you saw between legs and backpacks and purses; you remember how her toenails were painted as the bus bore you both through traffic and trees...

Lunch
(New York City, 1994)

Faces at lunch, oh, yes, smirking, lordly, bored or weary—here and there a flash of passion, of dreams, or loving seriousness; these signs I saw, notwithstanding the sweep of a fork like a Stuka divebomber, stabbing down into the cringing salads, carrying them up to the death of unseen teeth between dancing wrinkled cheeks;

a bread stick rose in a hand, approached the purple lips in a man's dull gray face; an oval darkness opened and shut and the bread stick was half gone! A lady in a red blazer, her face alert, patient and professionally kind like a psychoanalyst's, stuck her fork lovingly into a tomato, smiling across the table at another woman's face; everything she did was gentle, and it was but habit for her to hurt the tomato as little as possible; nonetheless she did not see it. Nodding and shaking her head, she ate and ate, gazing sweetly into the other woman's face. Finally I saw one woman in sunglasses who studied her arugula as she bit it. It disappeared by jagged inches, while across the table, in her husband's lap, the baby watched in dark-eyed astonishment. Her husband crammed an immense collage of sandwich components into his hairy cheeks. He snatched up *pommes frites* and they vanished *in toto*. When the dessert cart came, the starched white shoulders of businessmen continued to flex and shine; the faces gazed at one another over emptiness, maybe happier now that they had eaten, unthinking of what they had wrought.

From **Five Lonely Nights** (New York City, 1994)

He always sat in one of those chairs whose cushion was the color of canned tomato soup, in one of those chairs whose arms curved round to embrace your kidneys, at the table in the corner where the brick partition began. From this location (his loneliness reflected in the spoon) he could see one TV on a sports channel, bright and silent, and the two fans spinning circles of shadows across the pennants that hung from the ceiling like sleeping bats. Above the brick partition reigned the paintings: the ocean scene, the phony horse, the discreetly blurred nude, the happy child—and then was a wall of lace locked in place by brass posts. Through this he could occasionally find flickers of action from the bar, but he preferred to gaze down the length of the brick partition, past cash register and coffee pot, to where he could sometimes see the waitress who interested him. He did not love her; he did not know her name. But he was sorry whenever he didn't find her there. He had not yet learned when her shifts were because he did not come every day. Often enough she was there, blonde and Irish, rubbing her nose as she said something on the phone.

When she got the bone out of her throat and her ear out of her shoe, by then they'd hung up the telephone! a drunk was shouting.

On the television a man was in the driver's seat, closing the door of his car, and his arm was immense, bigger than his shoulder.

The door to the kitchen swung and glittered. He thought he saw his waitress's face through the diamond window.

She passed the small white table with two settings: two forks on the left, and a knife and spoon on the right, then salt, pepper, and flowers, always wilting flowers. He had never sat there. It would have been too sad to sit alone.

Some day he would take this waitress out to dinner and they would eat at that table. She would get up and serve them both, or else no one would serve them and the food would come by itself, sliding like the black plastic tray on which she brought his change, Lincoln's wry face uppermost, his edges curling upward toward the distant fans.

What's Your Name?
(New York City, 1994)

The long weary push broom whose dark bristles were as kinky as pubic hairs dragged itself attached to a man's arm and hand. It was very late. Two children sat drinking sodas and playing with straws and crying out: What's your name? —When the man's toil brought him near enough, they shouted their question at him in shrill excited voices. —Get Up Mess is my name, the man responded. That's what they call me. You make a mess and they call me get up mess. —The next man sat chewing gum and resting on the sides of his feet. —What's your name? called the little ones. —Sir, the man replied, his eyes shining like the cross on the chain around his neck.

Now it was ten o'clock in this tiled cave like an immense toilet, and the buses pulsed outside, and now it was eleven o'clock, and then it was midnight. The two children snored with their mouths open. Their mother's eyes closed slowly, and then a security guard came and shook her shoulders. The guard left the children alone. The buses all seemed to be either absent, gone, or out of sight. Half-asleep people queued or leaned. Only the escalators moved, winding remorselessly up and down like the treads of some monstrous tank turned turtle. A man fell asleep on the silver coast between escalators.

Not tonight, a ticket agent was saying to a sad man. Not unless you want to sleep in the terminal in Hartford.

Finally light burst out of a bus outside, and it sped away. Then in the darkness another bus came speeding, and he who waited and watched knew that she was on it, but then it kept speeding and was gone. A man sagged against the wall, curling his fingers against the side of his head, and slept.

Then suddenly another long bus angled in and upflung its sidehatch to unchoke itself of suitcases which were taken like medicine into the hands of people who then gave themselves to the emptiness between escalator railings and were accordingly transfigured, decapitated, unbreasted, waist-cut, knee-split, ankle-sliced, and then gone, leaving not even the soles of their shoes behind.

Another bus swam rapidly by, so that his heart rose and fell again.

He saw a sleeping woman who resembled her blurrily. The security guard shook her and she woke and looked into his eyes.

What's your name? he said on impulse.

Sweetheart. You wanna date? What's *your* name?

Gonorrhea, he said.

You sound like my type, the woman laughed. Let's go.

The security guard was still there, so he said: And what's your name, sir?

Fuck You, said the security guard.

Oh, said the woman. I guess he's my type, too. At least that's what all the men do to me.

He took her hand and they went out. —What's your name? he said to the taxi driver.

Go To Hell, the driver said, and he stepped on the gas and sped them straight there.

Pastoral Harpsichord

A house with a sagging porch
On the road to nowhere.
The missus naked because of the heat,
A bag of Frito Banditos in her lap,
President Bush on TV
Watching her every move.

Poor reception, that's the one
Advantage we have here,
I said to the mutt lying at my feet
And sighing in sympathy.
On another channel the preacher
Came chaperoned by his ghost
When he shut his eyes full of tears
To pray for dollars.

"Bring me another beer," I said to her ladyship,
And when she wouldn't oblige,
I went out to make chamber music
Against the sunflowers in the yard.

The Emperor

Wears a pig mask
Over his face.

Sits in a shopping cart,

A red toy trumpet in one hand,
A live fly in the other.

Hey, boogie alley Madonna!

I'm donning my black cape
And my orange wraparound shades

Just for you!

•

The Garden of Eden needs weeding,

And the soda machines don't work.

On the street of Elvis lookalikes
I saw the Klan Wizard in his robes.

I saw the panhandling Jesus
And heard the sweet wind chime in his head.

•

It's horror-movie time,
Says the Emperor.

Spiked hair, black flag of bug killers
In his belt,

He helps my frail old mother
Cross the street.

She's charmed and thanks him repeatedly:
"Such a nice boy,"

In the meantime,

Touching the mask's empty eye sockets
With her gloved hand.

•

On the graveyard shift,

Commands the Emperor.

Amplify the roaches crawling up
The kitchen wall.

Let's hear about their tuxes-for-rent places,

Their exotic dancers,

And their witch trials,

If they are the same as the ones we've got?

•

The child in a shoebox smoking
A black cigarillo.

The priest with a fly-catcher
At the altar.

The Emperor and the three-legged dog poet
By his side

Limping down the avenue.

•

Make us see what you see in your head,
We implore.

Okay.

He's climbing a ladder licked by flames.

He has a Liberace coat and a candelabra.

He's inside a mice cage admiring himself in the mirror.

Blow my nose for me, Cupid! he shouts.

He is playing with a million broken toys.

Sunset's Coloring Book

The blue trees argue with the red wind.
The white mare has a peacock for a servant.
The hawk brings the night in its claws.
The golden mountain doesn't exist.
The golden mountain touches the black sky.

A Dream Walking

p. 25: *Untitled*, 1991, color photograph, 8 x 10 in.

p. 26: *Money*, 1989, pants, gold lamé fabric, and clothes hanger, 44 x 16 x 1¾ in.

p. 27: (top and bottom) *Black Star Line*, 1992, mixed media installation, dimensions variable.

p. 28: *High Falutin'*, 1990, crystal candelabras, window frame, glass, metal, and wire, 130 x 58 x 13 in.

p. 29: *Dream Meat*, 1992, roasted chicken and bicycle pump, dimensions variable.

p. 30: (top) *Untitled*, 1992, copper, human hair, stone, fabric, and thread, height 60 in., remaining dimensions variable.

(bottom) *Flying Carpet*, 1990, Persian rug, fried chicken, and wire, 113 x 185 x 4 in.

p. 31: *Fragment of the Milky Way*, 1992, skull, human hair, bedspring, and flower, dimensions variable.

p. 32: *John Henry*, 1990, stone, human hair, and steel, 46 x 10 x 6 in.

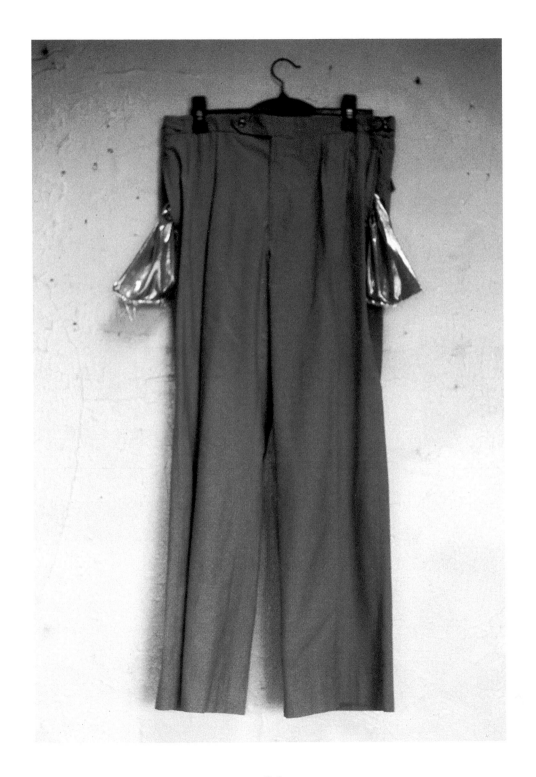

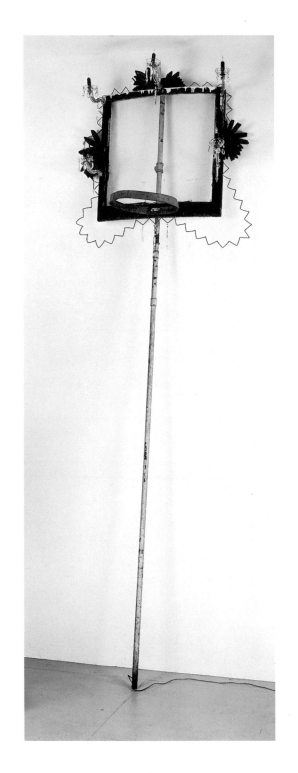

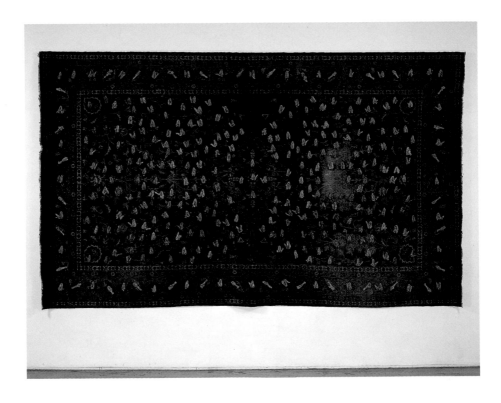

Duchamp As Iron Lawn Jockey

(For David Hammons and the nights at Vazac's)

E*nig*matic *Nig*ro
shivers in the *(coal)*.
Resourceful, industrious.
A credit to his kind.
Whyte ice-things
For Sale
on prayer mat:
snow*balls,*
snow*cones,*
snow*squares.*
Arming Santa(*n*)'s Elves
for the North Pole's
Jihad.
Pity,
he'll starve
and freeze
to death.

—Darius H. James

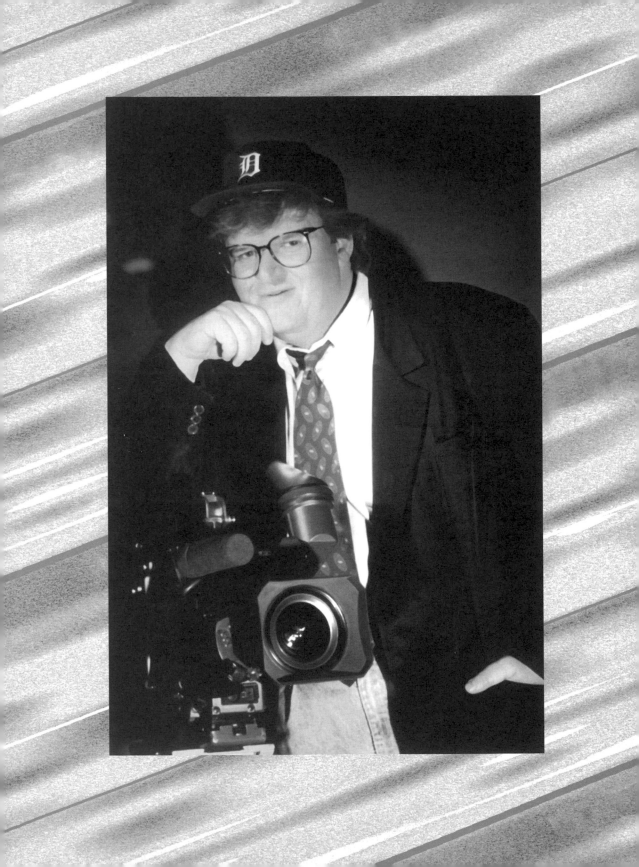

New York and Me

Petrolia/New York, September 19, 1994

ALEXANDER COCKBURN: Where are you living in New York?

MICHAEL MOORE: On the Upper West Side, Broadway and 84th.

AC: I always thought you were a regional roots man, who liked Flint, Michigan, and despised the tinsel trickery of New York.

MM: It's a lot like Flint. It's poor, noisy. The only difference is that you can see foreign films here. You can't see foreign films within an hour of Flint. And I actually do like all the activity.

Though I'm back there at least once a month, Flint's a hard place for me to live right now. It's hard for me to have much privacy there. The thing that's nice about Flint is that the people there are without pretension. What you see is what you get. But Flint lost literally tens of thousands of people, who moved away in search of work elsewhere. Each time I go back, there are more stores closed. It's becoming a shell of a town. You can see that here in New York, but on a much grander scale.

AC: Where do you go to work?

MM: They wouldn't give us offices at NBC.

AC: Quite right. Why would they want a scoundrel like you? So where are the offices of your satirico-politico-burlesquo-exercise in subversion, *TV Nation*?

MM: Down around Eighth Avenue and 49th Street. I take the Number 1 subway straight down Broadway.

AC: So you look at all the poor people and then... how many TV executives would you meet in a day?

MM: None. We had our own offices, separate from the network. The executives were all out in Los Angeles, and we virtually never dealt with them face to face unless I'd go out there. So we were very much left alone to do what we wanted.

AC: Who said, "This time you've gone too far!" Who was watching over you?

MM: There were NBC people responsible for the show and people in Standards and Practices. We dealt more with the legal department than anyone else. The biggest fear was that people would sue.

AC: In your anticorporate stuff, what made them most uneasy?

MM: That they would lose sponsors. But you'd give them a lesson in capitalism and explain to them that the sponsors really won't care so long as they're selling their products. The rope that we're selling them... you know what I'm saying. Actually I first read that Lenin quote in your column, back in Flint, Michigan. That the capitalists would sell the rope with which to hang themselves. I never read any Lenin or Marx, so my economic training was done by reading your column, first in the *Voice*, then in *The Nation*.

AC: How did *TV Nation* germinate in your mind?

MM: I was out in Los Angeles trying to get money for my movie, *Canadian Bacon*. I got a call asking whether I'd be interested in doing anything for TV. I said, "No, I've got to get my movie made." They said—this was NBC—"Come over anyway, let's see what ideas you have for TV." Then on the drive over there from West Hollywood to Burbank...

AC: On the drive. That's when all great ideas are conceived.

MM: I had to drive down Sunset to La Brea. I remember I had rock and roll on very loud. I thought, what would I like to see on TV? Forget about what they would like. What would I like? I started thinking about what really hasn't been done on American TV before: combining nonfiction with humor, giving it a political edge and a distinct point of view.

AC: So you parked in the lot, walked in...

MM: I met my agent and somebody from Tri-Star, the studio that would produce whatever TV show I came up with, before we saw the NBC executives. I told them what I was thinking, and my agent said, "Oh no, that's horrible. They're going to hate it." We went up and met with Warren Littlefield, the president of NBC Entertainment, and a couple of his v.p.'s, and I told them the idea and a couple of sketches.

AC: You thought of all this in the car?

MM: It was almost an hour's drive. That's a long time. And, you know, I've never done any drugs. Play rock and roll really loud and don't do any drugs, you can really get a lot done. I remember I had the ideas about NAFTA and going to Russia to look for the missile, and something on the Catholic Church. They were all laughing and saying, "That's great." And what do you know, when I went back to my hotel, there was a message from NBC saying, we'll give you the money to do a pilot.

What floored me was that I'd spent almost two years trying to get my film made. I started writing it during the Gulf War. It's a satire on the end of the Cold War. It's a comedy about how we're running out of enemies and there's no butt left to kick. The president needs an enemy because his ratings are slipping and the economy is in a shambles. He needs a war to divert people's attention, but not a real war. Since the end of the Cold War, real wars only last a couple of days. He says, "What worked for us was that forty-year Cold War when everyone was constantly scared shitless that the world was going to end any minute, but not a single shot was fired. All we have to do is create fear and they'll let us spend billions of dollars on armaments and we'll keep focused on the external enemy." So the president decides the best enemy would be Canada. It's close. It's there. They can devise many ways to make Canada look like the new Satan.

AC: Single-payer health insurance, for example.

MM: That. And then they own more property in this country than any other foreign country. Until recently, with the New Democratic Party, 53 percent of their people lived under Socialist domination.

AC: And they sent us Mort Zuckerman. But how do you tell them from Americans?

MM: That's the problem. Iranians you can tell. Iraqis you can tell, right? But Canadians!

AC: You could do a scene, like in the old *Invasion of the Body Snatchers*, where there are two fellows in the john and one says to the other, "Are you one of *them*?" and the other guy nods. In the Lebanese war, my brother used to tell me, an Arab would get to a barricade and the Phalangists would tell him to say some word like "tomato." And if he said "tom-ah-to," he was dead meat. There must be words like that in Canadian.

MM: "About" is a big one. They say "a-boot."

AC: Bang. Three "aboots" and you're oot.

MM: Three dozen different film companies rejected the script and told me the American public doesn't want anything political. I was on one of those trips trying to get the money when the NBC thing happened. So we made the pilot ...

AC: Wait a minute. The film, *Canadian Bacon*, is a satire on the premises of the Cold War: that strikes to the very roots of General Electric, which is an arms manufacturer. So General Electric gets its subsidiary, NBC, to ask you to do this show, thus distracting you from the really subversive thing, which is your movie.

MM: There's one more layer of irony that you're missing. After GE gave *TV Nation* the green light, it created an interest in me and my script. Two months after I shot the pilot for the TV show, I had the green light for my movie and two months later I was shooting it.

AC: Who gave you the money for it?

MM: Propaganda Films, which is a part of Polygram which is owned by Phillips in the Netherlands.

AC: Which is the deadly rival of General Electric. Furthermore Karl Marx's wife, Jenny von Westphalen, was a Phillips heiress. When things were tough for her and Karl, she pawned her jewels.

MM: Come on!

AC: Sure. *Das Kapital* was written in small part on money from Phillips. So you represent European capital against American capital. This is getting very elaborate.

MM: After I made the pilot and showed it to John Candy and Alan Alda, I got the money. I shot the film last fall up in Buffalo, Niagara Falls, and

Toronto. Candy finished it two months before he died. Then I got back here in 1994 and NBC said they wanted to do the TV show as a summer series.

AC: What's the reaction been to the show? Do people come up to you on the street?

MM: Whatever hopes of privacy I thought I'd get after leaving Flint... People are very happy about the show.

AC: Because it's anticorporate, irreverent?

MM: Most of the response, most of the letters I get are from people whose lives have been ruined because of their belief in the American dream. That dream went up in smoke somewhere in the last ten or fifteen years and they know they've been had. These people used to have fairly decent jobs, union jobs, and are now working for a lot less money, no union protection. Maybe they're working two jobs, maybe they're working twelve hours a day. They don't get to see their families very much. Some of them count as part of those six million new workers under the Clinton administration.

AC: We should note here that we are speaking on the first day of a glorious martial adventure in Haiti.... My theory is that they offered Cédras triple frequent flyer miles. That's what finally got him to agree to step down. Triple frequent flyer miles, for him and any companion of his choice.

MM: Yes, I've been trying to think, what was it in that last meeting... I've got this to say about Clinton. He's such a slime, but at least with him, President Baby Boomer, who protested against the Vietnam War and finagled his way out of it as we were all looking to do, I had the feeling that there was no way he would want to go to war. There are people farther left than Clinton who would have supported that war.

AC: Well, he did fire a rocket at Baghdad that killed several civilians including Iraq's leading woman artist.

MM: He'll do that. He'll do the Somalia trip, and he'll do other things beyond this, as they all do, to get reelected, or to get help in the mid-term elections. Right? Aristide was out for three or four years, so why, a month and a half before the November election, was it suddenly necessary to act?

AC: Have you ever met Clinton?

MM: No. I wanted to go jogging with him on the show and ask him questions while we were running along. They were so nervous! They actually considered it.

AC: I can't say you look too fit, Michael. Are you a secret jogger?

MM: That's what I said to Dee Dee Myers. If he doesn't like the question, all he has to do is speed up.

AC: *President Runs Away from Michael Moore.* Or *President Outstrips Michael Moore.* That's his headline. The first one's yours. You're running along Pennsylvania Avenue. What's the first question you'd ask him?

MM: Where are all the new jobs NAFTA was supposed to create?

AC: Then he'd come out with an incredible splurge of statistics that would throw you down on the sidewalk.

MM: No. I think he'd just speed up.

AC: Why do people, including you and me, hate him so much?

MM: At the core, people don't believe he's honest. Especially having someone from our own generation in there—he can't continue with that same line of bullshit that all previous presidents have relied on. A generation that grew up with Vietnam, with Watergate, etc., really should be treated with a lot more honesty. If he has such a low approval rating, that's probably at the core of it, regardless of where people fall on the political spectrum.

AC: He looks like a TV evangelist. That dome of hair.

MM: Yes, the hair keeps changing. It's going into a sort of Max Headroom thing right now.

AC: Back in the '92 primaries, I met a kid in Manchester, New Hampshire, who knew the fellow who cut Clinton's hair. He was obsessive, apparently. A little snip here to be JFK, then a little snip there. Anyway, back to your show. Dividing Yugoslavia up into bits of pizza, I like that a lot.

MM: I wanted to go in and, in a unique way, confront the men who were killing other people. Basically, I just wanted to get in their face and humiliate them.

AC: I love the mixture of politics and farce. Do you remember Renoir's *Rules of the Game* and the man dressed up as a bear?

MM: Of course. I brought the pizza in because I wanted the viewer to see just how absurd these men are, how ridiculous, how petty. How else can an average person fight back? I'm not going to commit acts of violence against them. I'm not going to Bosnia. So I thought of getting these ambassadors in Washington to divide up a pizza as if it were Yugoslavia. They took it so seriously, cutting it up, wanting this and that.

AC: Of course they took it seriously. They knew the eyes of America were upon them, not to mention those of their employers. Don't let that pepperoni sausage get over on their side, boy!

What about the accusation that you're laughing at ordinary people?

MM: Who are the ordinary people?

AC: I don't know. People trying to buy a house in Love Canal.

MM: The pieces I did tended to deal more with people in authority. As for the guy selling real estate in Love Canal, I think people felt sorry for him. On the other hand, ordinary people who become agents of the state and are doing bad things, what are you supposed to do with that? Political humor is a good way of providing a message—as opposed to giving a sermon.

AC: No, we don't want the sermon. Our side is always giving sermons and our side isn't doing too good.

MM: I don't think the sermon works. I really want to see change in my lifetime and I don't want to go to any more meetings at the Cooper Union.

AC: Cooper Union?

MM: I went there with you!

AC: The left's in terrible shape. Look at this jackass Bernie Sanders, the so-called independent socialist congressman from Vermont. He voted for the crime bill which is going to lock up every other black man in America.

MM: Why did he do that?

AC: First he said that if he hadn't, something worse would have come down the pipe.

MM: Oh man! Once you start thinking like that, they've got you.

AC: Change in your lifetime, eh? Inauguration of the socialist commonwealth, that kind of thing?

MM: Whenever they have a question down at NBC, I tell them I have to clear it with Havana now. It used to be Moscow.

AC: What would your first act as a socialist president of the US be? Mine would be the death penalty for all people riding motorcycles without mufflers. And as for you? Advance amnesty for you and your family...

MM: And triple flyer miles.

AC: The whole world wants frequent flyer miles. You want Americans sitting in front of their television sets to feel that there's someone out there sticking his finger up the nose of the corporations?

MM: Mainly I want people to think about some of the things we're bringing up and what they could be doing to get involved.

AC: But what can the poor buggers do? You should start a political party.

MM: Watching TV is one of the most passive activities you can engage in. So asking people to become active within the context of this passive activity is...

AC: ...a contradiction in terms.

MM: Right. So we may just be wasting our time. You know what I'd like to do? At the very least, if people come home after working for twelve hours, two jobs or whatever, turn on the TV, turn on *TV Nation*, if nothing else, if just for an hour, they can feel, "Yeah, fuck 'em." Just feel that there's somebody, some group of people that's on their side, that's taking on these bastards who've made their lives so miserable, and that we're not going to pull our punches, that we're going to stick up for you and you and all of you who have been shit upon in the past decade or so. If it's just that, whatever small bit of euphoria, whatever Bronx cheer, they can give the television set, I think that's okay, even if they do nothing else. Because I tell you, living in places like Flint, or putting out something like the *Flint Voice* as I did, "organizing" or whatever, you really do believe you're alone. You have no sense in this country that you're connected to a much larger group of people who share similar feelings. That sense of isolation eventually gets most people to cave in and give up. So if, in that one hour, people can have the sense that they're not alone, that there are people all over the country who are feeling this, and that we certainly support them, maybe that will help.

AC: Do you get different reactions from people in New York than in other parts of the country?

MM: Our lowest ratings are in New York. Our highest ratings are in St. Louis, Milwaukee, Orlando.

AC: Orlando. Let's keep that quiet. It's all those people who can't afford to get into Disney World.

MM: Let me tell you something: if Disney came to your town, how do you think you'd feel twenty years later? Mighty pissed off! We're big in Orlando.

AC: So why do you do so badly in New York? They're cynical. It's those relentless hours of being belabored by all those bullshit artists. They can't take anything in anymore.

MM: Very true. The tank is full and there's a lack of outrage here. At the network they're completely dumbfounded as to why the ratings are lower than in most other cities. They can't account for it. I tell them it's because the people who really bore the brunt of the Reagan-Bush years, and these two years of Clinton, live elsewhere. It's not that the people in New York haven't borne it, but the poor and the working class have somehow been manipulated into thinking that there's a leadership in this town that's looking out for their best interests and that this leadership is going to make things better for them. When you live in St. Louis, you *know* you're fucked.

We'll get letters from San Francisco, another low-ratings city, saying, "How dare you do that piece on Clinton and Hot Springs!* You have to support our president. We're going to have twelve years of another Reagan-Bush team if you attack our president." These are liberals who feel extremely guilty for having actually done fairly well during the Reagan-Bush years while millions and millions of their supposed comrades, the working class, didn't do very well. They don't feel very good about that. I used to get those questions after my film *Roger and Me*, why are you making fun of the bunny lady? Of those people in Flint? Well, first of all, I come from there. I didn't come from the Upper West Side and go to Flint to make a film; and secondly, if you're laughing at them, stop.

AC: How did the show do in Los Angeles?

MM: A little better. You see, Los Angeles has caved in. Liberal leadership means nothing. Who was the guy who ran for mayor as a liberal Democrat?

---

* This was a piece in *TV Nation* pointing out that despite the hagiography about Clinton's up-bringing in "a town called Hope," he was really from Hot Springs, a famous party town.

Well, fuck him! People didn't even bother to vote. They've had their collapse. This is just my theory, but we did better in places like that than in places where people are still living with the liberal illusion that things aren't as bad as they used to be. Boston's very good, Philadelphia is very good, Chicago is good. Washington is bad.

AC: New York, San Francisco, Washington, D.C., homes of the liberal elite. They don't like you much, do they?

MM: Not at all. The biggest attacks on *Roger and Me* came from Pauline Kael in *The New Yorker, Film Comment*, which is the magazine of the Film Society at Lincoln Center, and NPR. Now, with *TV Nation, The New Yorker* attacked me again, so did Tom Shales at *The Washington Post*, and there was a similar review in *In These Times*.

AC: What about the disposers of your fate, the NBC executives? What do they say about your politics?

MM: They don't care. They don't talk about it. All they care about is, can they sell time? Will people watch the show? I told them I think there's a growing despair in this country. The American dream went up in smoke and people are angry. People will connect to this show. And so we ran for seven weeks and did very well by NBC standards. It was the number-one-rated show in the 18-to-49 male age group, which is who they sell advertisements to. We didn't drop off between the first and last shows, we got more mail than any show in years, and they got better reviews. They were very happy. They were able to sell commercial time and when sponsors dropped out they were able to replace them.

AC: Did Ford advertise? Their CEO was able to change the oil in a car when you challenged him.

MM: I thought every working person, and nonworking person for that matter, would enjoy seeing me put the chairman of Ford Motors under a car and have oil drip in his face.

AC: He probably got a salary raise of a million a year for that.

MM: It's every shop worker's dream to be able to go into the head of Ford or GM and say, "Hey, get under there and change my oil!" You see, if you're working class you understand the sort of cathartic feeling you have when you watch that. If you grew up reading *The New Yorker*, you're not going to understand that. But that's okay, you're not supposed to. You have PBS.

AC: Do you read the letters that come in?

MM: I read them all. By the end, we were getting probably close to a thousand letters a show. In the last two shows we put up an e-mail address and we got 4,000 letters by e-mail. The previous record at NBC had been sixty.

AC: What's going to happen to the show? Are they going to renew it or junk it?

MM: They'll do something. They made too much money not to. I've never had a political discussion with these people. It's all about making a profit for the network.

AC: At some point it stops being about money.

MM: Don't say that yet! They'll read this. But you're right. That point comes. Hopefully you're the number-three-rated show and they have a horrible dilemma at that point.

AC: The world is strewn with the broken bodies of people who didn't think it would happen. Do you remember Sydney Schanberg? He's at *Newsday* now, but a few years ago he was writing a really good biweekly op-ed column about New York City for *The New York Times.* Everyone read it and said, this is great. For once someone is saying what it's really about. Then he wrote about some big real estate deals in New York in which friends of *The New York Times* publishers had an interest. Right away the window was open and the curtains were flapping and down there on the sidewalk was Sydney Schanberg. End of column. When they have to do it, they do it awfully fast.

MM: Reporters ask me, how do you describe yourself politically?

AC: On a scale from one to ten, I'm a nine! I'm a nine!

MM: My answer is, "I'm from Flint, Michigan." They go, "Huh? No, I mean are you a Democrat? Republican? Socialist? What are you?" And I say, "No, I'm from Flint, Michigan, and if you don't know what that means, I really can't help you out." Some people get it. A lot of the time they are people who grew up in their own Flint. If you grow up in the shadow of one of the world's richest corporations, and you see what that company did to your town, to your friends, to your family, you have two choices. Hopefully more of us choose my route, which is not to just crawl back within ourselves.

Once you've had the dream and then they take it away from you... You've been told that if you put your nose to the grindstone and suck in these fumes and work in this factory ten hours a day, then you're going to get this little cabin on the lake. So you work for thirty years. And then they come and say, "It's all over. We're going to Mexico and we're going to start all over again like we did here fifty or sixty years ago, and please give us the cabin back too." You don't have a job and you don't have the cabin. You're terribly angry and your anger is going to go either toward them or toward yourself. Unfortunately, the majority of Americans take it out on themselves, or their families or their neighborhoods, instead of going after the powers that be. So...

AC: ...here you are in New York.

MM: Here I am in New York.

AC: You don't think that secretly New York is going to hollow you out: you'll look like Michael Moore, you'll have all the appearance of being Michael Moore, but gradually Flint will drain out through your boots and a new entity will be composed. How are you going to combat that?

MM: First of all, I brought my wife Kathy and five or six people from Flint here to New York to work on the show. The core of the show is made up of my buddies from Flint. The choice was between here and Los Angeles.

AC: In Los Angeles, you wouldn't have to read *The New York Post* in the morning. There's a form of human liberation right there.

MM: There you go. I read all the tabloids every day.

AC: How can you stand it?

MM: I'm younger than you.

LOUIS FAURER

Photographs

Staten Island Ferry, 1946
p. 49

"Champion," 1950
p. 50

Accident, 1950
p. 51

Eddie on Third Avenue at 52nd Street, 1948
p. 52

Opening Night – Cleopatra, *Times Square,* 1963
p. 53

Untitled, c. 1947
p. 54

Untitled, 1950
p. 55

American Dream, 1948
p. 56

Photographs

For many years there seemed to be a curious open place in the course of American photography. Not a void, but a time without a central figure or dominant achievement. This roughly fifteen-year period between the Walker Evans works of the mid-'30s and Robert Frank's 1955 work *The Americans* has been best known in art as a time of high ground for American painters and sculptors, and it is only relatively recently that important photographic work from the '40s and '50s—by such as Levitt, Model, Siskind, Sommer, and Weegee—has become generally known and well regarded. In 1976, however, with shocking suddenness, I came to believe that mid-century American photography *belonged* to Louis Faurer.

One early morning in that year, through an encounter with photographer William Eggleston and the actress/writer Viva, I had the unexpected opportunity to see all at once the existing body of Faurer's work—four hundred vintage prints stored in his Chelsea Hotel room. Prior to 1955, Faurer's photographs had been prominently shown in such exhibitions as Steichen's important 1948 survey *In and Out of Focus* at the Museum of Modern Art, and his vastly popular *Family of Man* in 1954, but they had subsequently fallen largely out of public sight.

Where Evans and Frank were wide-ranging explorers, Faurer made only one important trip: from Philadelphia, his birthplace, to New York, where he stayed, and where his vision encompassed the all of it, both ordinary and odd. New York has been the major subject of Faurer's work, and the city is his natural habitat. He is at home, at one, with people on its streets, in its rooms. However serene or edgy his encounters, one senses Faurer (if one senses him at all) as having much in common with the people he depicts. It is a transcendent vision that allows him to *be* so many extremely varied "others." To restate what John Szarkowski has said well, while even the most literal of photographs are of facts, they must function for us (artist and viewer) as fictions. The people in Faurer's photographs (some order of humanity is almost always present) work as vivid characters in a sort of fictive drama, and a compelling sense of activity or situation can always be felt beyond whatever telling moment has been captured.

Over the last twenty years, Faurer has been justifiably rediscovered as a master of his medium.

—Walter Hopps

The Moron

We know what feeblemindedness is, and we have come to suspect all persons who are incapable of adapting themselves to their environment and living up to the conventions of society or acting sensibly, of being feebleminded.

—H. H. Goddard, 1914 (Director of Research at the Vineland Training School for Feebleminded Boys and Girls in New Jersey)

H. H. Goddard . . . on the basis of intelligence tests administered to 152 newly arrived immigrants . . . reported that 87 percent of arriving Russians, 83 percent of the Jews, 80 percent of the Hungarians and 79 percent of the Italians were feebleminded or below the mental age of 12—qualified, in fact, as "morons," a term originated by Goddard.

—The New York Times Book Review

On Monday Willi Wollen received the results of his test. He had been measured. The ceiling of cloud was low that day, coarse and hairy and flat, compressing the space of his world. The results came in with the daily mail. The envelope itself was undistinguished. Perhaps white. The alphabet employed to deliver the substance of this message was Latin, which is to say, ordinary; the numbers were within the normal range of positive integers, and were written unmistakably, in those Arabic numerals favored by Pope Sylvester II and now standard in the West. And the number itself—the precise number that described, in three digits (yes, Willi's I.Q. was very much in the three-digit range), the full extent of him, the features and quality, the topography, flora and fauna pertaining to his mental landscape—was adequate.

There have been lesser intellects, in the history of thought, than Willi Wollen's.

He had hoped, yes, that the number might be a touch higher—of course, this was vanity, and had no bearing upon anything, really—but he had hoped that the number might provide him with more . . . scope, that was the word. The range in which his number fell might have been more . . . auspicious. Thought Willi Wollen.

Immediately upon having this thought, he was beset by a nagging doubt: a doubt, it must be said, that young Willi never quite extinguished for the rest of his waking days. The doubt, if it could be voiced, said this: "Are you sure you are worthy, Mr. Wollen, of having a thought?" Indeed, thought Willi, was he capable, given the inauspicious nature of his number, of properly interpreting the result of his test?

For he had no doubt, Willi Wollen—of this he had no doubt at all—that the men (they generally were) who had devised this technique of measurement were of a considerably higher number than he was. Who was he to say what it might mean? One could imagine a greater intellect comprehending the world of a lesser, but hardly the other way around. The men who had tested Willi Wollen knew him, evidently much better than he knew himself, but he could not say—it would be hubristic to say—that he knew them.

Willi stopped and wondered whether he really knew the meaning of the word "hubristic." He thought he knew what it meant, but surely it had an entire wealth of connotation that was beyond him, given the nature of his number.

Because he shared most things with his girlfriend, who loved him dearly, and—the truth be told, admired him—Willi decided that he would present some of these doubts to her, so that she might massage them away, as she did with so much else.

"Um, what precisely *is* your I.Q.?" asked Willi Wollen's girlfriend, with a look of mild concern.

• • •

Upon hearing the results of his test, Willi's girlfriend remained silent. She did not say anything disparaging. She simply nodded—after a considerable pause—and then murmured a neutral syllable as she stared off at the low gray mass of cloud that held the city close. But there was a subtle change in her behavior, where Willi was concerned.

Once she had asked his advice on complex matters, and deferred to his opinion whenever a difficult judgment was necessary, but now she seemed to call on him to perform much less demanding tasks. "Willi, do you mind taking out the garbage?"

Willi naturally fell into this new role, because it accorded, in his mind, with his definition. His status. Willi no longer wished to be made responsible for serious thought, as it was clear that all of his ventures into that domain in the past had been suspect, and, in retrospect, probably fraudulent. "Willi, the sink needs scrubbing. Are you busy?"

At home, Willi began to notice that he did not really belong in the ranks of his family, which was a very accomplished family, in some ways exceptional.

A conversation between his sister, Kirie, who was fifteen, and his brother Jiri, two years older, confirmed his suspicions. Kirie was unusually excited at the breakfast table. As Mrs. Wollen poured cereal into a bowl, and Mr. Wollen lurked behind his newspaper—one of several that he read each day—Kirie bubbled over with early morning enthusiasm.

"Hey, I was brushing my teeth just now, and I was thinking about Fermat's theorem..."

"Fermat's *conjecture*," said her brother, Jiri, who favored precision in all things.

"Yeah, yeah, Fermat's conjecture," said Kirie, a bit annoyed. "And I was thinking, like, here's this monster problem that's been causing big fat math headaches for, like, *centuries*... and I decided: why not give it a little try? So I thought really hard, like, the whole time I was flossing, and guess what? I solved it! I found a proof!"

Mr. Wollen lowered his paper and flashed her a stern look. "Kirie, you're supposed to floss *before* you brush. You know that."

Jiri rolled his eyes. "You are, like, so out of it, Kirie. Fermat's conjecture was solved *months ago.*"

"It was?"

Kirie looked as if she were about to cry.

"That's okay, dear," said her mother, kindly, as she tended the toaster. "I'm very proud of you, anyway."

Kirie hit Jiri in the arm, hard. "You ruin everything."

Willi, who had been listening in silence, his spoon raised halfway to his open mouth, lost his appetite and left the table.

Everybody else seems so much fuller than I am, thought Willi. It's as if I'm just a story told in a human voice, whereas everybody else is a multimedia extravaganza, supported by fabulous and limitless technology. I want a video screen, thought Willi. I want my story to have at least that: a bit of high-tech support. I want to be modern.

As Willi walked through the bewildering maze of streets—Gramercy Park was, in fact, laid out in a sensible grid, but recently he had been getting lost mere blocks from his house—Willi stared at familiar objects with renewed ignorance. Do I really know, thought Willi, anything about buildings? Would I be able to make a house, were I given the pieces and the tools? He thought not. And towers: God, astonishing. His watch beeped, reminding him that an hour of his life had come to a fruitless close. He stared at the watch, deeply miserable, and knew that there were elements contained within the plastic case, tiny electronic wonders that were well beyond his sphere of comprehension. He might live two hundred years, and never understand the cheap watch on his wrist.

Whole systems of weather swirled around him.

Never before had he been so aware of the degree to which he was indebted to the intelligence of others. Other people, capable of thought, had for years buffered his life, creating a zone of comfort within which his mind appeared adequate: although he had never made an effort to understand much—say, plumbing or weatherproofing—he had always been under the distinct impression that he *could* have understood such things, had he wanted to. Only now did he understand the full distance of his exile from the inner world of things.

One of the clouds began to speak.

This was not an ordinary occurrence, clouds being generally

ineloquent, but who was Willi to question the workings of nature? Nature, clearly, had evinced little concern for him, when it ordained his place in the great chain of being. And so the cloud spoke.

It was a small piece of cloud, a yellowish puff with indistinct edges but a strong—one might even say intelligent—presence, which had broken away from the great mass above, in order to address Willi Wollen in person.

"Do you like my lining?" asked the cloud. "It's silver."

At this the cloud laughed, as if it had said something deeply funny, something that merited perhaps a rim shot, but Willi merely frowned. He *thought* perhaps he got the joke, but then jokes had so many levels, and he did not wish to betray himself.

"Watch this!" said the cloud, and it parted, briefly, to admit a glowing ray of celestial light. "Not bad, huh?"

"Are you speaking to me?" asked Willi, a bit nervously.

"Absolutely."

"I'm sorry. Um, who are you?"

"I am . . . insubstantial yet deep, amorphous yet perfect in design, individuated, yes, yet universal . . . you can call me Bob."

Poor Willi's head felt embarrassed.

"I am the Golden Cloud of Theory. Bob to my friends."

"Hi, Bob."

"Hello, Willi."

Two tiny creatures emerged from the surface of the cloud and danced across it, flickering across the silver like thoughts, or moments of electricity, or whirling storms. They were engaging; they were capricious and charming, and perhaps a touch vain. They would flash and then disappear, playing hide-and-seek in the thick outer layer of Bob, who seemed oblivious of their presence.

One was the color of copper and the other of tin.

"I am Ram," said one.

"I am Rom," said the other.

And then they spoke rapidly, and sometimes at the same time, so quickly that Willi's poor embarrassed head felt that it would like to disappear into his neck:

"I am Ram."

"And I am Rom."

"And Brian's on the Intercom."

"Be good," said Ram.
"Beware," said Rom.

And Brian on the Intercom
Said: "Please sign on
The water's calm."

"Boy there," said Ram.
"Boy gone," said Rom.

Deeply unnerved, Willi ground the ball of his foot into the pavement, and stared at his shoe, as if its grinding were an object of intense metaphysical interest. "I think I'm going to go now," said Willi.

"Don't be a spoilsport," said Rom.

"Don't spoil the sport," said Ram.

"To the sport go the spoils," said Bob.

They laughed, and Willi edged off, their laughter growing increasingly distant in his ears, until it was indistinguishable from the thunder, which cracked and boomed far off across the sky. A sheet of lightning spread briefly from one edge of the vast cloud to the other, and the world beneath it was illuminated sharply, but much too briefly to make any sense at all.

Guess I'll never know what makes lightning happen, thought Willi. He kicked a small object and it scurried off into the dark before he could figure out what it was.

And it was dark now, almost night beneath the sky, which was consumed in the density of storm. The first opening of the cloud above him, now, was not to permit a shaft of supernatural light, but instead to pour the weight of dense water upon him. The cloud opened like a gray bag tearing and emptied its wet guts onto Willi, who stumbled in the downpour, his clothes virtually useless as they held the water against his skin. I am naked before nature, he thought, but nature itself is clothed.

What a stupid thought.

• • •

Willi's girlfriend, after a long consultation with experts, determined that their relationship would suffer least if they were to dispense with the sham of having him educated. The ritual seemed increasingly nonsensical. After all, what was the point of pouring all this teaching into such a receptacle? It was like trying to tune a broken violin. Citing Aristotle, and how that very great thinker had determined that some men were by their nature intended as slaves, one of the experts convinced Willi's girlfriend that Willi's place in the order of things was to work so that she might be educated. Willi's girlfriend intended to go to Bennington, a very expensive college. She had been looking into a suitable place of employment for Willi, now that a college degree was pretty much out of the question, and had at last settled on an appropriate choice. It was going to be hard to present Willi at New York dinner parties ("My boyfriend works the salt mines..."), but the options were limited.

The next Monday, Willi reported to work. The giant crystals were beautiful, and Willi would happily have spent the whole day on his back staring up at them, but life was rigorous in the salt mines. Ideally, a miner was not supposed to appreciate the crystals in their natural state, as they hung from the rock like dark chandeliers, but instead to pry them from the walls with huge crowbars, and shatter them with steel mallets.

Willi did not like the prying, but what he really hated was to crush the lovely things. Even lying on the ground, rudely torn from their dark walls, the crystals had a measure of elegance. They were orderly but imperfect, as if drawn by an architect with a shaking hand, or designed by a flawed geometer, and Willi liked this imperfection, for reasons that are perhaps obvious: the crystals were, for Willi, evidence of an imperfect god. The kind of god that Willi might pray to, were he in the mood to pray to a god, but the stripes on his back put him in an almost irreverent state.

Willi hated to be whipped. Even worse than the bite of the leather into his skin was the moment of waiting, when the blow was still a vague whistling sound, an insect-like whine above his head. Sometimes the foreman would tease Willi, letting the whip crack against the cave wall beside him, so that Willi would untense his neck and back, after preparing terribly for a coming blow. And then, just as Willi had unknotted his muscles in relief, the whip would strike him in the soft place between his shoulder blades.

Willi was whipped more than the others, because he had a tendency to daydream. He would stare at the crystals, and soon he would be off in his own bright world. Once, the foreman caught him surreptitiously licking the surface of a particularly beautiful crystal, and Willi was consigned to the lowest level of the mine, where the pools of molten earth ruin your shoes.

And it was here that Willi at last began to question his position. It seemed unfair. I mean, Willi hardly thought that he deserved to be at Bennington, with his girlfriend, but surely he merited something more than this: the stifling pit at the very bottom of the salt mines, where the water that dripped from the walls was so hot that it left red marks on his skin, and the salt steamed in revolt against the humid air. Willi was sure that he could be happy with very little, but he did want something more than this.

"I want something more than this," said Willi, politely, to no one in particular. And then he shook his fist. "I am not a dipstick!"

The warm cave walls rang with this announcement, and a small puff of steam rising from the wet crystals began to take form, then speak in a familiar voice.

"Calm down, Willi."

"Bob!"

"Yes, Willi."

"I am not a dipstick, Bob."

"Man is a measure of all things, Willi, and you are a man. Therefore, in a manner of speaking, you are a dipstick."

"I will not be measured!"

"Ah, but you have been measured, Willi, and your measurements are not copious."

"I wouldn't measure you," Willi insisted.

"You are not in a position to measure me."

"Still, I wouldn't. I wouldn't do that."

"Well, that's a nice sentiment. But I think you should get back to work."

Overcome by a sudden impulse, Willi swung his crowbar against the rock wall and the bar rang, shivering in his hand. He swung it again. The bar tolled. The bell-like noise pealed in the cavernous space, multiplying in moist passages, until the air mourned like a cathedral.

Bob was concerned.

"I'm not sure you should do that," said Bob.

"I have seen man!" said Willi, as he beat the steel bar against the rock. "I have seen him. The depth of the black ocean could not contain the water in his eye. The length of the vast continent is not sufficient to span his cuticle. His mouth can hold entire stars, and does. I have seen him. Three times the height of the highest mountain measures the width of his single eyelash...."

The bar tolled, the cave rang.

"I have seen man!" said Willi. "In his lone torment, whole storms get lost. In his every thought, the lines of the universe shine like knives. I have seen him."

"Stop that," said Bob, but Willi continued to beat the side of the cave.

"I have seen man..." said Willi, but already the crystals about him were cracking away from their ancient foundations. "I have measured the span of his empty lung..." but the white crystals were falling, sharp boulders transparent and geometric, and as they fell they gathered others, until the sound of the tolling bar was lost in the avalanche of shattering salt. Willi fell and the bar bent beneath him.

When Bob described the body of Willi Wollen to his friends, he noted how Willi's death had seemed like nothing so much as the ruin of a good piece of meat, through the overzealous application of salt. What Bob did not see, as he constructed this clever metaphor in his expansive mind, was the part of Willi that flittered up through the steaming throat of the cave, winding and wheeling and falling upwards like a bat in pain. Willi Wollen left that cave. The sun glanced briefly, but with pity, on his crippled wings.

Latitude Sailing

It starts with the accident—the wind
    turns—the storm pushes the boat away
from the land it sees by—the men unravel
    cloth from rope, plank from water,
until there is only the similarity
    of water to water.
Maybe the sacklike shape of the sea
    becomes them, skin-blown, bones
traveling: some wreckage
    for your maps to discover. Or maybe,
without quadrant or astrolabe,
    unaware of magnetic variation,
someone is able (by luck, by forfeit)
    to divide the horizon and observe
the simple latitude of the sun afloat.
    The stars roll.
An obsidian island rises (somehow).
    Time passes in its own arc and
a disheveled boat rests
    in someone else's water.
The accomplishment is brief, unprotected.
    The weather will find them,
even if you don't. If they're lucky
    the habitable fabric of the world invites them in
before this happens,
    before the trees bow down or
someone reclaims the harbor. Either way
    they leave tracks,

footprints of wood or stone, a house-site, cooking pits, charcoal
    to pencil in the artifacts
of (your) ambitious imagination.
    But the relative position of lands, separated
by so great a distance and
    so many storms
was not found by Zephyrus or Boreas or Jesus
    or any conviction of paper
but by shadow and pole and the frailty
    of a guesswork crossed by need
or just by the simple gyrations of cobwebs.
    You wanted to know how it was possible,
to sail from island to island
    without any lines to guide you,
without the solid ground and blind
    comfort of directions.
But you can still run down the parallel
    (as they did) with nothing
but the meridian altitude of the sun
    (maybe a lodestone) to point the way—
because the problem of navigation
    isn't the lack of directions
but that the end is never where it's supposed to be.
    Without the feel of the line
the birds still find their migratory tracks
    and the whales still blow you where you want to go.
Maybe the map is the skin of your hands
    or the hide stretched
around the spokes of your impossible boat, or
    maybe the hope of finding
what you want to see is greater
    than the sixteen winds and sixty-four points
that was all they had.

Maybe just the evidence
(four fragmentary iron rivets,
    one ring-headed bronze pin, one arrow head—Dorset Eskimo—one
                                                    fragment
of bone—pig—unidentifiable bone fragments, etc.) is enough for you
    because it is all you have.
In the Arctic summer, between dawn and just after sunrise,
    when air rests on a much colder surface,
what you see can be optically displaced
    upwards from its true location
and you can see
    objects—islands, mountains, someone else's boat—
that are far beyond what the horizon should give you.
    Imagine (in someone else's horizon)
your own boat so disheveled:
    how do you see, how does anyone
plot the accurate course
    with the stars dissembling and the ice-floes
overtaking themselves and the icebergs calving
    to their own impossible dimensions and
you (now,
    in a temperate climate, without your maps and with some failing
                                            imagination and no
    stars) are nowhere to be seen.

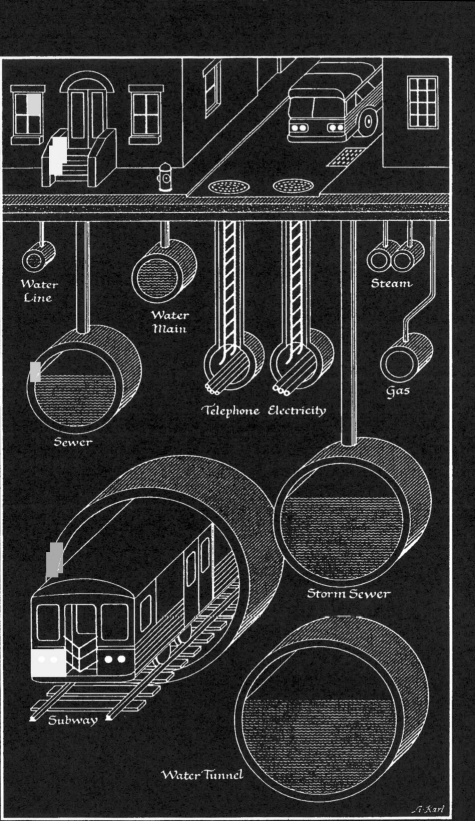

Voices from the Tunnel

Journal entry (April 1989)

Each venture into the tunnel brings about the same feelings: as soon as I hit the stairs and start down into the darkness, I feel that I am entering something dangerous. I suppress this anxiety, fear, and hesitation partly because I am getting to know the people there, and partly because I know that I am writing this book. Even when the tunnel residents become my friends, the fear is still present every time I go down. I realize now that the fear is not of the tunnel per se, but of something inside me. Entering the tunnel evokes a primal state in my being. My antennae are suddenly alive. I am acutely aware of all that is around me: the rats underfoot, the rocks falling, the strangers who might jump out of the darkness at any time. There are points of sheer darkness where I can't see my hands—a momentary derangement of the senses so far removed from what I felt five minutes ago as I walked through Riverside Park. That's when I develop this notion that the tunnel is the unconscious mind of the city.

Early Research Plan

The environments in which I hope to conduct research include tunnel spaces where the homeless sleep, eat, and/or stake out a claim. I will investigate three research sites: the 168th Street subway tunnel, under Grand Central Terminal, and 72nd Street to

125th Street below Riverside Park. I intend to map out territory behaviorally, to interview tunnel residents, and photograph their dwellings, cardboard homes, rafter homes accessible only by ladder, and burrowed homes under train platforms. Over the past four months I have established ties with seven tunnel residents, one church, two police precincts, and several social welfare agencies serving the tunnel areas of West 72nd Street and Grand Central Station.

Field notes: first descent into Grand Central (April 1991)
We began around noon making our way down into the many levels at Grand Central Terminal. We put on those orange train reflector vests that the engineers and workers wear and started walking toward the tracks. It is clear that one needs to wear these things because there are many trains moving in all directions. I crossed twenty-one third-rail electrified tracks during the two-hour tour and many times felt totally bewildered by the sheer complexity of the maze-like structure. We encountered the loop of circular tracks where trains can turn without having to back up. We moved down from the second level and about twenty-five feet above the tracks there was an extended bridge-like structure, a grate of some sort just hanging there with newspaper, magazines, and cardboard covering it. The sergeant calls it a "nest."

Field notes: Nesting
The "nests" can be dated by looking at the newspapers and magazines that line them. Most are only several days old. Some are built in "colonies," where clusters of people live together in groups of twenty to fifty, men and women but no children. Plastic-filled garbage bags act as pillows. One nest we see, spread out under one of the steel pillars that supports the Waldorf-Astoria, is made up with almost military precision. The ends are tucked in and the blankets are smooth. At the head of the bed is a small metal chest that holds toiletries. Ten feet away from the spot is a private elevator made by the United States Secret Service for Franklin D. Roosevelt. Apparently he was brought from Hyde Park, New York, in a private train car, then wheeled into the elevator and up to the hotel.

Tunnel resident's dream (April 1992)

"Dream tonight was about a mushroom tea that a friend told me to take so I could be healthy. She said it would help my kidneys, help my heart, help my liver and other parts of my body. The tea is called *kombocha*. It tasted like vinegar but I wanted to try it by myself so I went home and this is where the dream really starts crazy. When I came into the tunnel the whole place was bright and full of light, not dark like I know it is. My place here was bigger, with rooms all over, and I tried to get some sleep but I felt like the mushroom had gotten into my body because I touched it early that day. I felt the tea pulling me out of bed and it was a powerful force like I never felt before. When I got up in my dream and went to the kitchen I could smell the tea all around and I saw this bright light come in through the window that I don't have. The tea materialized into a woman with powerful hands and small feet. She walked up to me, kicked me, and patted my head. She said she was sorry and kissed me passionately. At that point two dogs arrived on a postcard with the inscription: Tunnel dogs."

Metro North Official (April 1991)

"People tend to think or believe that there is some vast underground chamber and that people are lost down there. Every nook and cranny has been searched by us. We know every place a person can hide. We've heard the beauty-and-the-beast stories, the alligator-in-the-sewer stories, but this place is more labyrinthine in myth than reality."

Research notes

Prior to the arrival of the railroad in the mid-1800s, the Hudson River area was a community of squatters. By the 1930s, when City Parks Commissioner and master builder Robert Moses covered the New York Central railroad tracks, creating a two-and-a-half-mile-long tunnel under the promenades of Riverside Park, it had evolved into a shantytown. Eventually the tunnel was no longer used for rail traffic and current residents began moving into the space as early as 1974.

In 1990, approximately 113 tunnel residents were found by Amtrak work crews, who were renewing track in the abandoned tunnel for passenger train service between Pennsylvania Station and Washington, D.C. Sensationally depicted by the media as "mole people," these residents refused interviews with the press or other representatives of "topside" society. They designated a spokesman, "Glaucon" or "The Lord of the Tunnel," to speak for them.

Journal entry: descent below Riverside Park

Jumping over a four-foot brick wall, I walk down a sloping dirt-covered incline with evergreen shrubbery on both sides, next to a winding S-curve in the West Side Highway. I squeeze through a short fence before passing through a hole in an oval, latticed iron gate in Riverside Park and from there into an almost infinite black expanse. Inside I see a platform structure extending down a pipe-fitted banister with rickety steps. A few steps down I hear a man say, "Watch out for the next step." It is the person I will later call Glaucon, a thirty-seven-year-old black man from Florida. "Walk along the edge," he instructs. "Grab hold of the steel pipe and jump over the next step."

A tall, dark-brown-complexioned man, he refuses at first to say his name. He says that what people call him is of no consequence. "I don't live there [in society], I live in this dark community. None of us have any real need for names. We are no-names. This whole space down here is the land of the unforgiven."

I walk the remaining steps onto thousands of hard rocks, scattered against miles of glistening rust-colored tracks. Autumn leaves, yellow and brown hues with specks of green, are falling through a grate directly in front of me. In the fall, people begin moving from streets and subways to tunnels. This tunnel is like an asylum with a concrete sky, a sanctuary from the chaos above ground.

Glaucon speaks in a professorial manner, forming words carefully, educating as we move along. He speaks intelligently about art, science, and poverty. He refers to Shaw's celibacy and Melville's fidelity as though rationalizing his life underground. He tells me he has Robert Caro's *The Power Broker*, Kierkegaard's *Either/Or*, Kafka, and other books cased in the cartons in his bunker. And his biblical allusions are too numerous to mention. "Hezekiah," he says, "who was the thirteenth king of Judah, lived and built tunnels in 700 B.C. He built them right in Jerusalem. By that alone we are in good company. We have no reason to be ashamed of our tunnel existence."

He takes me to meet other residents: a Vietnam vet and a woman with whom he shares his bunker; his friend Alibi, a spiritual man who believes his crackhead wife is into *magica*; his con-man friend Kal, who spent half his life traveling the country as a short-order cook; the Cubans at the south end; and Kovacs, the oldest man in the tunnel, who hates blacks and was once offered a movie deal for his life story. These are only a few of the more than one hundred dwellers in this community, and only a handful of the more than 5,000 documented tunnel people in this city.

Tunnel resident (April 1991)
"'Hello' is the worst, worst word in the language because the minute you say hello, you invite grief."

Field notes
Many underground residents do not consider themselves homeless. They are, as one woman put it, "temporarily without shelter," and they consider the subterranean chambers of the tunnel a safer housing alternative than city shelters. Inhabiting a harsh ecology, deprived of water, natural light, food, electricity, heat, they struggle constantly to protect themselves against cold and dampness. Some live in the cinder-block structures originally used by railroad

personnel that can be found along sidetracks. They live high within tunnel embankments, inside wall niches accessible only by thirty-foot ladders, or build free-standing structures in the tunnel's dark recesses.

Pet cats are highly valued as predators against rats. There is a communal kitchen, where meals are prepared on a fire spit positioned under an air-vented grate. Water, food, and firewood are gathered outside the tunnel from construction sites and barges along the Hudson River. The setting is visually powerful, the horror of these living conditions lit by a cathedral-like shaft of light. Graffiti extends throughout the tunnel. "Home of the Queen," at the 83rd Street and Riverside Drive entrance, is a reflection of the gay activity that takes place there. "Donnie 3-10-90 Rest in Pice" records a tunnel resident's death from AIDS. At the north end of the tunnel: graffiti replicas of Dali's clock, Michelangelo's David, the Venus de Milo. Much has been vandalized, not only by teenagers, but by Amtrak workers to assert their dominance.

Journal entry by Glaucon

I am thirty-seven years of age and have been a resident of Riverside Park's tunnel for six and a half years. On May 17, 1985, I asked myself what I considered to be the ultimate question that one would ask of oneself in life, and the answer was simply that I know myself completely and totally and that I seek and make true contact with the universal mind known as GOD. Being one to allow logic and reasoning to govern my existence, the task seemed very simple. I must simply dare to be myself. With the understanding according to the word of GOD that I am nothing and that I know nothing, logic would be my key to all understanding. It is truly my belief that it has become the nature of man to be stupid because he refuses to deal with the simplicity of things.

On June 7, 1985, I descended the staircase of the tunnel and felt vibrations of an alien nature. Listening to the inner voice, I turned to my left and walked about 500 yards north and observed some concrete structures, eight in number. I decided that this would be home. Knowing that this level of existence was truly new to me, the inner voice said, to get where you want to be you must first accept where you are. And what appeared to be my lowest point was truly my highest. So my mission began.

Field notes (August 1993)

In the first four months in the tunnel Plako and Bobo never slept without interruption for more than five hours at a time. But of the twenty-four hours in the day, sixteen at least and sometimes more were spent in sleep, with three of those hours spent dreaming. In the last six months of being in the tunnel, they slept twelve hours on average with three hours of dreaming.

Life story by Robert Kaliroki ("Kal")

I was raised in Chicago, Ill. I am one of six children. I have two brothers, one is a cop and one is a priest. My mother went to church every day for over fifty years and my father worked at one job for more than forty-two years ever since he came to the United States. I never got along with my mother because she was always on my brother's side—the priest. And my brother the cop, well, we had nothing in common, he was much older. But the only good thing about my younger days is my father [who] always took me to the zoo. That was my best times, to get away from home. I would feed the pigeons, he would drink. But he could hold it more than anyone I knew. But my father would never go against my mother about me. They would fight every day but they were married fifty-two years till my father died. I did not know about his death till six months after he died. I don't talk at all to any one of my family.

At age nineteen I got married to a girl from Ireland. She was something else. But as everything in my life, it did not last very long. My wife's family had money and she was the only child. One day she said to me that we were going to go back to Ireland. I said I did not want to go. So she took the child and went back by herself. I really was not in love at that time. After that I joined the air force. It was then that I started drinking and doing drugs. I loved the feeling of being high. I was always one step in front of the next person. After I got out of the air force I started cooking. But by that time I could never hold a job very long, because if I was high I just wanted to party. After a while I gave up the booze but started doing pills twice as much. All I wanted to do is stay high no matter what it took. I would stay up two to three days at a time, sleep for six to seven hours, and start all over again. People did not want to be around me because I could be very warm and then very cold.

After ten years of pills I started to travel. From New York to

①

Mr. Robert Kalinski Life Story

I was raised in chicago Ill. I am one of six children. I have two brothers, one is a cop + one is a priest. My mother went to church every day for over 50 years. and my father worked at one job for over then 42 years. ever since he came to the United States. I never got along with my mother's life because she was always on my brother's life the Priest. And my brother the cop well we had nothing in common. he was much older. But the only good thing about my younger day's is my father. I always took me to the zoo – But my father would never go agenst my mother about me. they would fight every day but they were married 52 years till my father died first. I did not know what his death till 6 months after he died. I don't talk at all to any one of my family. I never talk to my mother since 1964. she is dead now. At age 19 I got married to a girl from ishland she was some thing else – She was a mona's Girl But I did not know that till it was to late. She had a daughter 11 years old But as every thing in my Life it did not last Very long.

L.A. or San Francisco every six months. I lived in every city in California. I lived like that for twenty-five years. All this led me to become homeless. I became homeless in L.A. then I found the Salvation Army. Being a cook, they put me in the kitchen working. I was doing very well but always thinking about the pills. One day the captain came in and told me he was going to put me on payroll. I did not want that so I left. I started selling diet pills. I had twenty-five doctors to get them from. No one ever knew where I stayed and I did not trust anyone. I never sold to kids. I only sold to bartenders and owners. They paid the most. Things started getting bad for me so I went to six drug programs but never finished. Maybe I did not want to stop. I came back to New York. I started cooking at a soup kitchen where I met Glaucon. We became friends. We cooked together for about six months and he told me that anytime I needed a place to come and see him. Well one day I did. In the winter 1986 at eleven p.m. All he said was here is a bed, it is yours. I've been there for six years.

Journal entry
Glaucon spoke about seeing somebody crossing the tracks. I looked over his shoulder, saw nothing. A few minutes later, he mentioned another image, coming up the tracks. Again I turned to see nothing. It was now clear to me, after six months, that he was suffering from visual hallucinations.

   "Did you hear about my old buddy Rick James? I'm not one for gossiping but I knew about the coke thing from way back because I used to deal to him. He's gone overboard with this base thing. He's probably done all those things they say he did. And Michael he's always had an identity problem. Not knowing whether he wanted to be a boy or a girl. Again this coke thing, people don't realize what they're doing with this drug."

• • •

Death by hallucination. Death by hallucinatory smoke.

• • •

In a city as vast as this one, there are many realities, many truths. What I put down here is true to my observations. It is the trick of perspective that I speak of here. It holds fast until someone else comes along and orchestrates a different look-see at the people who colonize the night. My night eyes see and decipher the rhythms of street life and offer a slightly different focus than others, just as my diurnal eyes occasion a new truth.

Conversation with Glaucon (April 1991)
See rats again, a pigeon nesting near the top of the girders, think I see a bat too. I meet Glaucon near the 90th Street entrance and walk into the darkness. Can't see much for a few minutes. Finally,

we sit down at the fire-spit area and converse on a range of topics from God to Nietzsche, neither of whom I know much about. Glaucon does most of the talking. My grandmother said once that I had two ears and one mouth—so talk less and listen twice as much. I guess that's what I'm doing today. The weather is on the cold side but the tunnel is quite serene. I'm beginning to enjoy coming down here. It is less chaotic than above ground. Glaucon goes into his house, which he has not allowed me to enter yet. I have not asked and he has not offered. He keeps saying his place is a mess. I end up counting the insects in the earth, looking for *Spirobolus marginatus* (millipedes). I stop digging when he comes back out. He wants to talk about the kids who have been in the tunnel for the past few days causing problems.

"I can say without hesitation that the only ones I hate are the kids who come down here and paint on the walls and deface the nice work that Zane and Chris have done for us. The kids have tried to destroy all of the art and that's why I'm going topside tomorrow and buy some paint to have it retouched. I guess you heard about the homeless guy sleeping down at the end of the tunnel who was burned to death by a bunch of kids. They just poured gasoline over him and lit a match. You know the kids are at fault, but don't it make you wonder what kind of parents they have to do such a thing? And I bet they will just say they were having fun.

"My place was set on fire too last year. It wasn't kids that did that. I know who did it. It was jealousy that tried to burn me out. I know where the person is and everything and when I get myself together they're going to get theirs. You mark my words."

Field notes (May 1991)
On the wall at the far end of the tunnel two blocks away from Kal and Glaucon's place is what they refer to as their living room. Several graffiti pieces appear on both sides of the tracks. One is a modern Mona Lisa and the other is of Ted Williams. Both have been marked by anti-artists. A bright orange penis has defaced the mouth of the Mona Lisa and a machine gun is sketched near Ted Williams. The space is near the entrance where gay men meet to consummate sexual acts. Kal and Glaucon have taken to cleaning up the pieces and want to do so with the help of anybody who can give them a dollar for spray cans.

Journal entry by Kal

I'm out there every morning every day of the week. I go from 110th Street to 96th Street east side which is my Sunday to Monday days. Then I go up from 110th to 96th on the west side on Tuesday and Wednesday. Crisscrossing every day, you know, they put out the blue barrels with the cans. Depending on which days you can do good, you know, if you know where they're putting them out and there's not a lot of guys picking them up. Sometimes there's a beef from somebody, but most of the time it's okay, especially if the super likes you. A super helped me today because I was putting the cans into a little bag and he brought me a 50-gallon bag and said, "Here." I make myself twenty dollars in four, five hours.

Journal entry by Alibi, a windshield cleaner and ATM panhandler (April 1991)

My name is Allen but everybody calls me Alibi and I've been down here two years. I came from North Carolina and I've been in New York for thirty-one years. I know you want to know how I ended up here in the tunnel and without a home on topside. Well, I was like everybody else topside. I thought I was immune from any bad things happening to me. I had a job working in an office and I got married to a younger woman. She was very pretty but about a year into our relationship she started using crack. One day I come home and she's getting high and I tell her it's me or the crack. She said she didn't need me as much as she needed the drug so I was all fucked up. I was devastated by that shit. I went to my job and took all my stuff out of my drawers and started walking. I walked around for days and I ended up talking to a friend who said people were living underground here and I could go down and see what was happening. I did that and I ended up spending the night. I went to look for work, but after a while I couldn't say I was living [at home] anymore and I couldn't say I was living down here, so I started selling books and other things on the street. One of the things we do down here is look after each other.

You see how I came over to check you out because I'm also a little pissed off at the journalists because they put my name in the paper and they say I live down near 72nd Street. Well, if they say that then my friends topside will know that's me, because how many Alibis could you have around 72nd Street? You tell me.*

Journal entry (July 1991)

Saw Kal's place today and it was an awful sight, filled with cups and cans, broken glass, and a small table with drug paraphernalia. Glaucon took me there. He was angry at Kal because he said he stole the tape recorder I gave him to record his life story. I'm not always inclined to believe people when they say these things. I guess if he stole it he sold it for money to inch his habit along. Glaucon says Kal is strongly addicted to crack, cocaine, and amphetamines. At any rate, they both play such games I wouldn't be a bit surprised if they are in tandem with this little charade. After all I gave Glaucon another tape recorder after he misplaced the first.

The other week Glaucon calls me to say they need a lock on the east entrance to counter the Amtrak officials who had sealed the entrance shut with a padlock. Kal called the next day to say they needed money for a lock and chain. The money is never much to speak of so I don't see the necessity of such contrivance. But the $17 which is insignificant to me may be more to them, particularly if they are putting together many such small-scale scams.

After I received a call from Glaucon, I went down with the photographer to see what it was about. I had not been there for some three weeks and wanted to check on the flora and fauna as well. I picked three different kinds of apples, one apple tree by the 89th Street entrance and two along the West Side Highway. Then I walked a bit further to find an assortment of crab apples as well as elderberries and cherries. I tasted all of these fruits before walking down to 72nd Street where a huge fence—at least twelve feet high—had been erected since my last visit.

Conversation with Kal (March 1991)

"You got good guys and bad guys down here just like you got everywhere. When we first came down here the people who were here didn't create any problems and we in turn let some people stay down here. One person we let stay was a woman who was raped

---

* Alibi is a pseudonym.

by two guys we knew but didn't know. You know what I mean? I mean we saw 'em down here but we didn't have much to do with them. We just met 'em once or twice. But the fucking guys come down and rape this woman and then try to get away and we caught them and turned them over to the cops. That was our good deed for the day. Naw, for the fucking year. Those two fuckers are in jail and we helped put 'em there."

Field notes (March 1991)
I changed my clothes twice to help battle the cold down in the tunnel. No matter what I wear, I get cold after an hour or so standing, walking, no matter what. Kal asked me to meet him topside at ten o'clock but he was nowhere to be found. Decided to go and call him through what Glaucon refers to as their intercom. It's the grate on the West Side Highway. It's a little risky to walk out in the curving highway traffic, bend over and scream fifty feet down at someone you can't see, but I did. Saw Kal after hollering a few times, his face staring up from the floor of the tunnel. I walked about two blocks along Riverside Park, parallel to the highway to get to the entrance. The first thing he started talking about was the rats. He was walking ahead of me and I couldn't quite make out what he was saying because of the gravel underfoot and the cavernousness of the tunnel itself.

"We had an epidemic of rats about a year ago around the grill area," I think he says. "We just couldn't get rid of them. We didn't know what it was, you know. We don't keep food around. We keep it where they can't get at it. They was just, you know, they just congregated. And of course we got some cats down here fast and the cats took care of all that. Like I said, it's been a month now since we heard anything out of the rats."

Journal entry
There are so many odors competing for the olfactory sense: the tobacco, sulfur matches. The butane has no discernible odor, but it is one of the hidden poisons flowing down to the lower body parts, penetrating pungency, crack's partner, the freebaser's lover. Marijuana, when it appears, takes precedence and after it, tobacco.

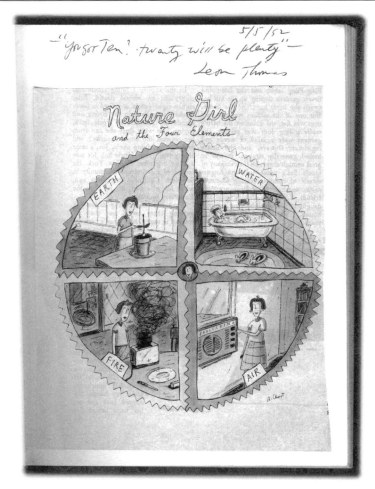

Tunnel resident "Nature Girl"'s note to T.W. (May 1992)

You are a CooL or a GooD con man. I am Puerto Rican woman, 28 years old, 5' 6" height, 130 weight, 2 children, dancer. My name is Doreen. My real name is Ada Lus Roman.

Conversation with Kal (March 1991)

As he talks I feel the cold wind burst through at us. We move closer to the outside area called the kitchen. The floor of the dirt kitchen compound extends about 130 by 30 feet and is a pot, pan, and can environment. The spit, a steel divider from a stove, is fitted over bricks and is blackened by wood smoke.

"A lot of good meals come out of that fire. A lot of good meals." Kal's face is etched with a thousand wrinkles, not so much from old age, he says, but from stress. A train zips through, on its way to Washington D.C. Dust flies all over us. Kal squints, holds up his middle finger, and says, "There goes my dignity, man. There goes my dignity."

"The train," says Kal, "is the worst thing that could have happened to us because it brings so much of the outside world into a space we have considered our own for a long time. We get along with the Park Police from the 24th and the 20th Precinct. The police, they all know us. But the Amtrak Police started coming around and bothering Glaucon one day. They had nothing to do but try to make things bad for him and me. They would come around one or two p.m. and make all kinds of noise. One put his hand on his gun."

Research notes

Some people initially acted crazy to avoid talking or interacting with me or anyone above-ground, only to later act sane when they learned through the tunnel grapevine that I was okay to talk to and wasn't somebody "crazy from topside." In many instances they apologized.

The growing literature on homelessness has excluded systematic study of tunnel populations and the impact their harsh environment, mental problems, and drug abuse have on how they survive. In many ways, tunnel residents are pioneers in an urban frontier of time and space. In the transformation members of this community must go through, from life above ground to tunnel life, there is a spiritual bonding. Tunnel residents have joined with the underground.

Tunnel resident's note to T. W. (April 1992)

It's cold here: This is the way I feel some days. 'Cept I can't find a black dog whose ass is bigger than mine. Any idea? Hope Europe is a gas. Just don't bring back any greasy-looking sandals like the dude on the left—and no high-water poly pants like the dude on the right. Also, don't catch any social diseases and by all means don't fall in love with anybody your mother wouldn't approve of. R.

Journal entry by Kal

The tunnel was not easy. Every day to get water you had to go half a mile to get it and half a mile to bring it back. Glaucon and me used to get five to seven days' worth at a time because you did not know when it was going to rain. Another thing is food. We had a school three blocks away that gave us the food at the end of the day that the kids did not want, but summer was the worst.

Also the media. Some were good and some were bad. The worst was the *Daily News* who said we were "mole people." I don't look like a mole person and neither does Glaucon. CNN helped us I think the most. They helped us to stay where we are at now.

I know everything will come to an end within one or two years. After all this is over I am planning to go back to Chicago to live. I have not been home for thirty years. I need to find love again. But will not know what to do with it when I find it. I will have to adjust to being up *top*. I think I will be a better man. I grow a lot. I respect people. My life is what I made it. Nobody got me here and no one will get me out but me. When I do move I will be a lot more real than I was for over forty-five years.

I hope no one will ever have to go through what I did to live. I will try to live one day at a time, do one thing at a time. Writing this has helped me look at myself in a mirror. I never hurt anyone but myself. That was big for me. I hope God will let me live a few more years so I can go back to my past instead of running from it. Writing this I feel all alone. Maybe because I am.

MARGARET MORTON

The Tunnel

The Tunnel

One of the oldest surviving homeless communities in New York City stretches for two and a half miles underground on the Upper West Side. Hidden from public view in an abandoned freight tunnel, this habitation existed for sixteen years before it was discovered by Amtrak crews renewing track for passenger service between Pennsylvania Station and Albany. Most of the residents of the fifty-block-long community refused to leave, and the population has continued to increase as the more visible homeless encampments are demolished by the city.

The earliest tunnel residents live alongside the tracks in cinder-block structures originally built as storage facilities. More recent tunnel dwellers have built plywood shanties or perched themselves on narrow ledges. Shafts of light angle through air vents. Dwellings are clustered around these points of entry and on the light-washed walls are images and writing left by grafitti artists.

An underground water source was shut off in the early '80s. Tunnel residents are now forced to walk miles below and above ground to obtain water and food. Meals are cooked over fires that also serve to combat the damp chill. Residents recycle the discarded furniture and cookware of nearby apartment dwellers to create their own homes, and take into their care abandoned pets.

—Margaret Morton

Aubade on East 12th Street

The skylight silvers
and a faint shudder from the underground
travels up the building's steel.

Dawn breaks across this wilderness
of roofs with their old wooden storage tanks
and caps of louvered cowlings

moving in the wind. Your back,
raised hip and thigh
well-tooled as a rounded baluster

on a lathe of shadow and light.

Red Sauce, Whiskey and Snow: A Still Life on Two Moving Panels

Ingots of cinnabar and gold
Under a window of snow
Snow-sky, ganglia of dark branches claw up at it
Olive-skinned Tina soaks in the tub
Snow along the Hudson, fastening to stone the length of the Palisades
Falling on valleys and abandoned pavilions at the river's northern reaches
The kitchen light almost amber, Dutch Interior light
The little green vase, stone Buddha and indigo cat, backlit on the windowsill
Through the window wild diagonals of snow
Blowing across planes of snow
Gables and sweeping roofs, shadows, brick and an enormous crow
Sponging her swarthy aureoles small vesicles appear
The ferry slips through the snow, back and forth to Manhattan
The towers ghostly as it pulls away from shore
A gathering aroma of earth and fruit
As the sauce darkens with the juices of meat, craters and thickens
Somewhere back there, early in the second movement
The clarinet located an emotion, one long forgotten
Then let it go
Drifts have nearly buried the pumphouse
And a great quiet has covered the swings and jungle gym
The suave bit of oak, an unfastening, a tap at the base of the skull
The slow release of sibilants, o's and l's
Then thunder, muffled, snow thunder, no
A big jet passing by low, hidden in cloud

Rain

Up in that part the water smelled rivery. We hadn't even passed the little bay at the end of the first beach but already the air was touched by the promise of our destination. All the trees were drowning. They reached their long skinny branches into the lake, leaning so far that their gnarled roots could barely hold the clay. You knew it was only time before whole bodies would be dislodged, allowed to drift, then sink. The water would seal over them again and that's how it would end: you would never know there had been trees there at all.

There was a glut of water at the lake, miles and miles of fresh water wash spread over the curve of the earth with no horizon of land you could see. Still the rivers and streams ran into it, still-melting snow off the mountains sluiced the blue channels dark with cold. Every year the water levels rose. Water crept up higher and higher on the sand, another lump of earth was crumbled away. Even on the road you could see signs of its advance: pumice crumbled in the gutters, green weed stains on the tarmac from where the lake had flooded in spring. It came from building on a land spit, people said. You couldn't claim it gave you real foundations.

As the beach curved away from the few pale, wooden houses that marked our summer town it disappeared. If you wanted to walk that way, past the drowned bay and beyond, you had to wade and then climb up onto the grass, pushing through the thick clusters of lupins that grew there. Your hands parted the tough yellow blooms that closed again behind you like a seam, the warp and weft of heads and stalks unbroken. It wasn't until you came over the other side of the rise that the growth thinned out, back to scraggy grass again, frilled at the edges with sand.

Further on, past the bushes and up and over the rocky hump at the end of the first beach, the sand swept wide again. Low cloud came in over the lake in the mornings and in the pale, thick light the water, lapping on the white shore, was like cream. Swimming out into it you could feel how with each stroke you were further and further into whiteness, folding into the air like an angel.

"Don't go!" I heard Jim crying, far away. "Come back to where I am, it's scary there."

Strange, he believed I would leave him when he was the one who was always trying to get away. He ran from me as soon as we reached the second beach, springing ahead onto the wide tablet of sand like a little dog let off a lead. He ran in great sweeping circles, around and around, backwards and forwards from the water to the dry.

"I'm over here! Look at me!"

My elastic boy.

What was the need in him that carried him from me yet kept him to be within my sight? Later I found out that lovers did this, had the instinct to be solitary while wanting glances, touches to ensnare them. Was he like one of those? A trained creature who could swoop away yet was retained by an invisible thread? What was it that took him out, brought him back, took him out again and left him? His voice looped now, lightly over the quiet air, floated.

"Hey..." he called. "Watch this..."

Over at the edge of the lake he was throwing tufts of pumicey sand into the water.

"Take that!" he flung another handful, and another. "Take that! And that!"

The sand sprinkled like sugar on the surface. He watched it for a minute, delicate, then was off again, spinning along the moistened rim of the beach, picking up a stick and dragging it behind him, leaving a mark that dissolved as fast as it was made, then dropping it and running off again, released further and further into distance until he was just a seed.

He was my younger brother by seven years. James Edward, born 1967. Jim Little, my mother called him. "Because I'll never let you grow..."

She had lots of special names for people, she jingled them around until they became habit. "You can be 'Petal Pie' or 'Sweetie,'" she said to me. "But don't forget your Daddy's always 'My Boyfriend'..."

On the days when she stayed in her darkened room, when she was sick or resting, she didn't use the private names. It was more a thing for parties or a cheerful mood—putting her makeup on as she dressed for the evening, or chasing my little brother fresh out of his bath, wearing her yellow bikini.

"Come here my little fishy tadpole, I want you for my supper!"

He slipped away from her and ran out the door, naked and shining.

"You can't catch me..." He danced around on the buffalo grass that grew outside the house, the lake tilting golden behind him as the sun went down.

"Put on your pajamas and come to bed, Jim Littlefish." My mother held out a blue towel to trap him. "Come in now or I'll cuddle you to death..."

Our parents had parties all summer, they started at dusk and went on deep into the hot night. The lights were on in every room, spilling out onto the lawn, and the music from the record player was turned up loud. *Love, love me do. You know I love you. I'll always be true. So ple-e-e-ease. Love me do.*

The adults loved the songs, they sang along and danced. If you'd walked past our house at night, hearing them, seeing them together in that way, you might have thought: I would like to live there, be pressed up with them against the windows. You might have wished your mother was as beautiful.

The dawn would be ashy with cigarette ends when Jim and I came downstairs in the morning. People were sleeping on the sofas, spilt food around them and the empty sound of a record spinning in its groove. There were bridge parties and cocktail parties, and petrol barbecues when my father charred dripping steaks over a naked, leaping flame. No matter how much the house was cleaned afterwards, the smell of meats always lingered. Sometimes I believed I could smell it on our skin.

For all those summer holidays Jim stayed little, he never seemed to grow. It was like my mother's spell had come true. He remained miniature and perfect, a tiny bird-boy with a tracery of fragile bones and shoulder blades that stuck out like wings.

"Come on! Hurry up!"

His voice carried across the warm gray air. No urgency was conveyed by it, how could it be?

"Hurry on!"

I was never fast enough for him. I was too much of an older sister, I suppose, walking behind, making perfect footprints in the sand. There was a faded T-shirt I wore that made me feel like a teenager. When I reached him he was sitting down, legs crossed, drifting sand through his fingers. I could have put my arms around his whole body and contained him there, neatly as a parcel. He was tanned dark from the sun, tumbled like a stone to smoothness. But for his soft cotton shorts he was bare.

"Don't do that!" He shook his head away when I wanted to place my hand on his silky hair, feel how warm it was, how it smelled of sunshine and sand and clean water. "I'm not a girl."

As we came further along the beach the depth of the lake fell away, receding into distance. At first there were only rivulets and small puddles stranded on the wide sand, ridged patterns of waves left dented in the wet, but as you walked on, getting closer to the river-mouth, you could see that water coated the beach entirely in a thin film. Here was a plate of water, a tray, where you could walk out for miles toward the horizon and still be no deeper than your ankles. Clear fish darted in the shallows like electric currents and if we stood quite still they came right up to us and kissed our feet with tiny fish lips. Nothing bad could happen. There were no hooks to catch or lines to bring you down, no deep ledges or treacherous currents could tug your body away. The sun shone, diffused behind the layers of mist and gauzy cloud, and Jim Little ran out upon the lovely shining skim, sparks of water charging up from his heels in a spray. The gray light opened around him, at my back condensed. The water loved my brother too much.

It was a strange freshwater tide that had slipped over the beach and done this: the river. Twice a day it caused the lake to rise and fall, disgorging water into water when it was full, spreading across the sand when the level was low. From out of the cleft of bush it came on, a slow deep plow of water carving a smooth passage between the hills, wanting to change. As you came closer you saw how dark the water was, how complicated by shadows from the overhanging growth, how the jade insides of the water were flecked with gold. Trapped below the water's surface, hanks of pale blond weed washed endlessly downstream. It was so quiet you could hear the water sucking around the strands, so quiet you could hear bubbles of air forming and breaking, the soaken air trying to breathe.

No one knew how far up the river went or what the country was like in the place where it came from. You could travel upstream for miles, for days, for weeks, my father told me, and still find yourself no closer to the water's source. The river would continue, quiet and knowing, while all the time you went deeper and deeper into the country, the colors of the bank changing from orange to yellow, clay to dun, rocky and wet with leaves in the parts where the sun never got to it. There would be a place where vines would wrap themselves around the rotting tree stumps like terrible old lovers, their ropey arms strangling anything else that tried to grow there. Wild pigs might come and snuffle you out, or a deer would step from the shadows into a clearing, blinking in the light. With every step you would find yourself covered with thick brown dust from the ferns, your skin might be bruised and torn. Perhaps the bush would be cleared, in parts, into scrubby farmland with a few mangy sheep. A dog may have barked outside a hut made of sheets of corrugated iron, rusted red and black, and maybe someone lived there, or maybe they were dead.

I guess a thousand, a thousand thousand rivers must have run into the lake, trickling threads of water, slim deep channels, waterfalls and rocky rapids breaking their surface so violently that watching them would be like watching glass breaking over and over, in thunderous pieces and shards and sprays of white, white powder. Yet, with all those rivers pouring in, adding water to water, charged with fish, thick with twigs and leaves, from where they had broken off the hillsides way upstream and drifted down, only our one seemed to have contained within it all the places it had been.

"Let's go and discover..." I turned for Jim Little, with his facemask and damp hair he was meant as a child for rivers, and realized he was gone. Suddenly emptiness was all about me. In the still water, silence; in the carved trees no breath.

"Where are you?" I heard my voice go out into nothing. "Where are you?" I started to run. Already he was slipping away forever into the second of his leaving. "Where are you?"

How my awful voice pierced the opaque sky, sent out alone for his returning. "Where are you?" it cried. "Where are you?"

The cry came back from the hills empty. "Where are you?" it echoed, quieter now. "Where are you?" As if the hills could have saved him. Their massive shoulders rose straight out of the water, the darkness of their reflection cast like a cloak about them. Old mothers, they had no children.

From way off there, out on the thin lake, he heard me, turned, hesitated for a minute. Then he saw me, started to run.

"Wait for me!"

Behind me the hills rose, the sky was darkening.

"Hurry!" I called. There was no time.

"Wait for me!"

"Hurry!"

"Don't leave me!"

Now he runs towards me and I hold it, that minute. I own it. The silver sheet of water trembles about him as he comes, running back to me through the light air. I cry out—a sound, no words. My youngest, smallest brother... For five years he occupied my life, all his movements, his few words, mine. The lovely bend of his fine limbs was the dream I had for my own body, to be light and careless and, with no heaviness of speech and thought, in endless, continuous motion of flight. Even today I think how my brother, running out of the low milky cloud, his cotton shorts a blur of faded red, is me. It lasts a lifetime, that moment of him coming towards me. His whole self, mine, is caught up there in that particular combination of muscle and bone and skin and hair. And how strange it is that, for the complexity of it, for all the gathering up that there was in his running, when he reached me it was as if he had simply stepped out of the air to be by my side. "Hi," he said and he took my hand.

There was a jetty near the mouth of the river, not very big, where everyone kept their boats. It was sheltered there. The stilts sank deep into the still green water for strength and even in a high winter wind the boats would be safe, bumping their white and painted sides gently against each other, tucked away from the lake's great expanse. To get to the jetty, you had to follow a narrow path that curled from the open beach into the bush. In there, for a few steps, you were surrounded so closely by growth that you could have felt stifled by it, the way it pushed in on you, surrounded you with its dark odors, but then you turned the corner and suddenly you were out by the river again with the wood of the jetty worn smooth under your feet, boats bobbing on either side.

We had a small sailboat tied up there, though nobody used it. Jim and I weren't allowed to take it out on our own and our parents rarely sailed, but my brother and I liked to go and sit in it anyway. Although it was moored to the wooden pole, tied and trapped, the sound of the water slapping against its sides was enough. If you faced out toward the river you didn't see the other boats moored on either side and it was like you were the only ones on the water, alone with the silent green ahead of you and dark infinity beneath.

I stepped in first and felt the little yacht lean into the river, then regain its balance. I reached up for Jim where he stood on the jetty and lifted him in. He was light as bone. I sat him down beside me and the water barely shifted beneath us. Sometimes a heron flapped down and landed on one of the big rocks at the entrance of the river or a bird shrieked out of the bush, but these were the only sounds. We could sit there for hours if we wanted, we were so generously alone. There might be a biscuit we'd eat, that we'd brought with us, or a plum, but mostly we were still. We were dreaming, I suppose. Making plans for leaving. I thought about all the places we could go in the boat, how we could escape the summerhouse forever. Our father, badly sunburned with his poor pink eyes, could line up the glasses on the table for cocktail hour and we'd never have to see him. Our mother could be sick again, bringing up those animal sounds, and we wouldn't hear. In our boat we could be safe, quite sure of our destination. It was where we needed to be. As we sat together, the green water before us turning slowly opaque as the clouds deepened, a trout completed—with one leap—a splash, a silver curve. Everything must change.

When the rain came it came first as the scent of rain, the gray air stained darker behind the hills. Then when it came down to us it was like thread and needles, piercing the jellyish water with a trillion tiny pricks, the silver threads attaching water to sky. And there too was the sound of rain, drumming gently upon the canvas cover where it was stretched taut at the back of the boat. It was so warm.

Rain was with us, all around us and in our hair, wetting our skin, trickling down my neck to the center of my body. Drops of water hit the enamel cup that was there from the days when our father kept all his fishing things in the boat, the bag of knives and hooks, his covered rods. Sometimes my mother used to go out with him. The two of them rose early when it was still dark, like lovers they left the house and ran across the lawn. The grass may have been damp with dew or dry from night after night of hot moonlight, warm beneath their bare running feet. They must have pushed the boat out in those days from the beach, there was no need then to keep it tied up and trapped, they would have pushed it together, fumbling with the ropes in the dawn until the wind caught the sail. Then, in seconds, they were off, swept across the water, night at their backs and the sky paling before them, the light carving out a space around their young faces.

Neither my mother nor my father went fishing anymore. The rain hit the enamel cup with a tiny musical sound, striking the cup, filling it. Drop after drop, the rain. If it rained long enough the cup would be filled with new water. Out across the river rain fell, from behind the hills, rain. Rain into water, rain on leaves. Raindrops dripping from the white blossom of the trees, rain sliding down the muddy channels of the riverbank, rain on us. We let it do that, cover us, the sky could weep. My little brother tilted his face up to the last of the light and closed his eyes. Under water he was transparent.

• • •

Your blood is full of air, as is your body. This is something you should know when treating your patient. Don't let the other things sicken you, the slimy touch of skin, the piece of weed extending like silk from the nostril. Get on with your job. You know what to do.

Before beginning any form of artificial respiration it's necessary that you first make sure you can hear no breathing. Lay your ear close to the open mouth, look deep inside it. Remember, at this point you may feel no pulse, at neck or wrist there may be no signs of life, but this is not to say the patient is dead. Even doctors sometimes have to hold a tiny mirror, a glass, above the lips to be sure. If you are outdoors it is unlikely you will have accessories like these; you must rely instead on your own senses. Is the chest moving, even slightly? When you bend over the face, can you feel the lightest breath against your cheek?

If there really is no air at all you must act quickly. You have no idea how long this body has been unconscious; even if you took him from the water just seconds ago it takes only a very few minutes for the brain tissues, deprived of blood flow and oxygen, to die. After that the nerve control that keeps the body alive will fail. Strong swimmers, of course, who have rescued in the water, are able to give mouth-to-mouth resuscitation between strokes, so lessening the possibility of unconsciousness once the victim is on the beach. The reality of enacting this life-saving procedure however is more than difficult. Panic, fearfulness, the instinct to put speed above all other priorities in getting the body to dry land . . . these factors will tend to overwhelm. Even the most experienced swimmer could find that he or she is actually pushing the head of the victim under the water as she swims. Afterwards, that person may imagine the victim gasping, mouth wide open, attempting air, before being submerged again and again in the waves. More likely it was the swimmer's own breath that was heard.

Despite this, and irrespective of whether or not this kind of rescue has been attempted, the first thing to do on shore is to get the patient on his back. If there are obstructions in the mouth, clear them. Do this by scooping with two curved fingers, reaching as deeply into the cavity as is possible to remove debris, blood, vomit, mud. Additional matter lodged far back in the gullet can be removed by the forefinger alone using a hooking action to 'flick' back hard objects: small pebbles, for example, shells, a plug of sand.

As soon as the mouth is clean you can proceed.

Bend the head right back so the tongue cannot block the air passages and cause choking and suffocation. There are several ways of doing this. The safest is to press the head with the heel of your hand resting on the forehead and your fingers on the bridge of the nose. Alternatively, you can adjust the neck by placing a hand beneath it and lifting it upwards. The set of the body, once out of the water, will tell you whether or not you should adopt this handling position. Is there an unusual displacement of limbs, for example? A twist to the pelvis? Is the neck turned at an unnatural angle? Any of these would indicate that there has been severe battery in the water and so alert you to potentially serious damage to the spine. Be so careful. Make sure the neck is well aligned by the pressure of your own hand but do not attempt under any circumstance to rearrange the arms, the legs. Your patient is not sleeping—and besides, there is no time now to make him lovely.

Once the throat is extended, the head back, the airway is then clear to breathe. Occasionally spontaneous inhalation will begin at this point, the patient reviving in a matter of seconds. If this is not the case, immediately commence artificial respiration as detailed below.

At the softest lower part, around the tiny openings of the nostrils, pinch the nose shut. Use the same hand you have pushing down on the forehead to do this, with your other hand pull the jaw open as wide as possible. Of course, when the muscles are limp and the head thrown back the mouth will fall open naturally, but the extra hold you have on the jaw, your fingers tight around the chin, will act, slightly, as a vise. Know this as a safety precaution. Should there be involuntary spasms of the body, the head is kept safe. Even so, take care as you grip the chin that your fingers do not interfere with the mouth. You need it clear for the next step.

If, during all this time, you are alone and while you are handling the body in this way, you may wish to shout for help. It's your instinct, a thin thing, and of no use. If the beach is empty calling is hopeless, you know it. Though it may seem that hours are passing by, really these are minutes, seconds. That drip from a strand of your hair falling onto the forehead of your patient, that's real time. In the lifeblood of anatomy it's eternity. Your shouts, calls, if the day is misty and there is no one about, are in vain. Emotion cannot dictate action now. It's what you do that brings life, not words.

Concentrating then fully on the task at hand you may use your thumb to bring the patient's head up to increase the air passage even further—but don't let your hand press on the base of the throat. This is the windpipe, and a delicate organ for bruising and damage. Think of it as a soft reed, an instrument. Any pressure on this young part will stop off all breathing and, with the victim already in a state of deep unconsciousness, it is doubtful you would even notice.

Therefore keep the area quite free, open to the air. Let the light play across it. For a minute, see the whole body, the form of it, resting weightless on the curved sand.

Now you have him.

Inhale deeply then and seal your mouth around the patient's open mouth. Can you feel your lips pressing as if on a cold wound? Can you be sure no air can escape around your lips, are they widely apart, fully covering the opening? Blow then, but gently, be gentle with him, blow into his mouth.

"Aaaah..."

There is your sigh, your old life, sounding in his cave.

"Aaaah..."

Fill his lungs with your sighing, your expiration. Make your own inhalation as rich, as deep as possible. Do it.

"Aaaah..."

Again.

"Aaaah..."

As you do it, as you breathe into him, his chest will expand and then you must immediately take your mouth off his so his lungs may expel the air that you have breathed into them. Is this clear? Are you understanding? Four deep breaths into the mouth, the chest filling, then expiring, filling, then expiring. No matter what your thoughts are at this time, the sequence of your actions is vital. Count, one—two. Count, three—four. Don't let yourself be persuaded to hurry nor should you linger. These first four breaths you give him are so important, don't wait for the full flattening of the chest between each. Oxygen is vital now, you have to get as much oxygen as you can into the lungs. Don't be afraid to blow as deeply as you can; the air you breathe into him is from your mouth and windpipe only, there are no poisons in it. The small amount of carbon dioxide from your lungs is too small to be toxic. You can't harm him further. You can't, with your breath, do damage. You're giving him oxygen, keep remembering that. Oxygen for his blood, his watery heart. Oxygen for his brain, the tiny nerve ends wavering like anemones. Oxygen for his eyes, feet, hands. Oxygen for his whole body running lightly, a wisp.

"Don't leave me!"

There was a glint on the water, a call in thin air. Don't think about that.

"Help me!"

Don't. It's too late. You can't hasten him into life with your panic, concentrate on what you're doing. All of it, each crumb of a second of it.

Breathe in, one—two.
Breathe out, three—four.
Breathe in, one—two.
Breathe out, three—four.

This is real. Put your finger at the pulse of his neck. Can you feel it? That little beating sac, bird's heart? Is it alive?

Certainly if, during these first four communications with the patient, matter rises in the mouth as you breathe into it, a recovery is more than likely. Breathing has started and now the channels are sluicing themselves, readying the passage for regular inhalation and expiration. Simply sweep out the contents of the mouth using your fingers in the method described earlier, remembering to place the head on one side so the liquids can drain. You're one of the lucky ones. Others, facing no such signs of life, must immediately commence the next phase of recovery.

External chest compression can be seen as a violent act, instigating the circulation of the blood by making the heart pump artificially. To make the compression you will be depressing the breastbone onto the heart that lies behind it, forcing the blood out of it and into the arteries. When the pressure is released the heart can fill up again from the same veins. To perform this on a child is not easy. Applying such weight to a smaller torso can easily cause damage to the ribs and internal organs, and for this reason, for the reason of a framework of bone and muscle that is softer than yours, there must be some alteration of technique if you are not to cause rupture and bleeding. Therefore you will be using one hand to make the compression instead of the usual two-handed method applied to most adults.

First, make sure the patient is on a hard surface—so as to provide support at the back for the moment when you come down hard upon the chest. Then feel quickly along the breastbone for the exact point on which to apply pressure. If you imagine the length of the ladder of bones as being divided into three sections, the part you need to find is two thirds down, where the second and third sections meet. The child is thin so you will have no problem locating the relevant part of bone: you can see it articulated there beneath the whitened skin on the chest. Put the heel of one hand on the point there and, keeping your arms perfectly straight, lean forward, push into him, using the weight of your whole body for pressure.

Don't bang or thump the bone. The anatomy of a child will be traumatized enough by the sheer weight of your body leaning upon it. Don't you think you're doing enough? Were the situation in this instance less grave you would not even contemplate compression. The body is too small. As soon as you have come down on it release your weight. Immediately drop back, still kneeling. Leave your hands in position. Now you will see the breastbone rise, and for a split second will believe the cold boy is breathing. Once he appears to have air in him, lean down again and press upon his chest as before, as if you were forcing all the breath out of him once more.

For someone acting alone, this is not easy. You must work more swiftly on a child than on an adult, continuing with artificial respiration as you do so. Start off by making the compressions at the usual rate of eighty per minute but quickly increase this to 100 per minute. After the first fifteen compressions give two full mouth-to-mouth ventilations, follow this with a further fifteen chest compressions, two mouth-to-mouth ventilations . . . and so on, in sequence, quickly, regularly. Keep going, don't stop, keep pressing, keep breathing. Fifteen compressions, two ventilations, fifteen compressions, two ventilations. Keep going, keep going. Where is your time now, there is no time.

Whatever is happening around you, don't stop. A crowd may have gathered at your back, there's disturbance in the air, perhaps they're talking to you—don't hear them. You're trying to get the heart beating, the chest breathing spontaneously again. Keep checking for a pulse. You've already felt at the neck after the first four ventilations, if there is nothing there, if, as doctors say, "the pulse is absent," keep on with the chest compressions. One minute later feel again, feel for the lightest beat of blood through the artery there, it could start any minute, and if there's nothing check again and keep checking, every three minutes from now on, press the shallow dent on the throat with your finger, any minute now, any minute. If the heart has begun to beat, if for a fraction you hear it, or if there is a pulsation in the neck artery, stop the compressions immediately. It would be dangerous to continue pumping the heart artificially when it has already found its own natural rhythm. Put your finger there again, did you only imagine you felt it jump? Whatever happens, whatever you pretend, don't stop breathing air into him. You know a heart can beat for a few seconds, a pulse quicken, but without an involuntary intake of breath it's only a phantom coming alive. Breath, that's what you're waiting for, the first harsh gasp for air. That's your sign, that's what your own heart is racing for. Air for him. Air in his body. A disgorge of water from the mouth and air to breath, cloud, light.

What do I need you to know now? How long to continue? You know the answer already; people don't stop this thing. After minutes even the panic is gone and what is left to you is process: the eye on the second hand, the finger at the throat. It's process, it's what you're doing to him now. Compressions, counting, your mouth on his mouth, your hand on his head . . . It's process, process. You don't stop this thing. Even after the others have come and pulled you off him, still, you don't want to stop it. He's yours. You took him from the water. You know what to do. You've been with him there all along, before someone on a boat saw you, before people came. Before they called the doctor, before, you alone were all his company. You were the one natural with the body, all the time it was you. Your lips around his cold lips, your hands around his wet head. He was yours. All the time you knew what to do.

Water-rescue manuals and first aid books claim grand successes, line drawings show it: Grown men and women propped up like happy dolls, contented recovery positions from now on. In theory the aim is to continue with resuscitation until the patient is breathing normally again—perhaps after several hours of both mouth-to-mouth ventilation, external chest compression and a combination of the two.

"Carry on without interruption and use any bystanders to send urgent messages for aid and an ambulance."

In the picture it arrives, inside, two friendly men with blankets.

"Loosen any tight clothes that may be constricting the patient, keep him warm . . ."

"At this point, if it is to hand, a little brandy can be of use . . ."

You'll turn pages and pages of recoveries before they tell you the truth about time. Continue, continue. That's how it starts. Any minute now, the pulse will catch, a breath, you'll hear it. Continue, you can cheat on time, aren't all book deaths just pretend? Continue, and you turn the page again.

"Continue until you are prevented from doing so by a doctor or someone experienced or in authority," that's what the book says now. "Even when all the correct techniques have been applied... Even when compression appears to have had some success..."

You turn the page.

"Many patients whose heartbeat and respiration stop can never recover..."

You turn, you turn.

"...At the onset of the incident this cannot be foretold."

Come away now. Leave it.

"Even when..."

"Even when..."

Leave it. There's nothing you can do. You know at the lake there was always too much water.

Even in dry summer, water. That part of the country was a carved-out bowl for rivers running to it, rain. My father could predict the floods and freak storms in their thick cloud colors, yellow for thunder, indigo for lightning. It was geography, he said, the cold plunging depth of a volcanic lake and the warm air banked up around the mountains. Marriage in the way they attracted, in the way water banked up and had to break. We swam in water that changed color by the weather. See-through for the hot days in the shallows, pale chiffon-blue deeper, dark underskirts beneath. Other times, when close storms held the lake still as black glass you could believe it might bruise you... Then the wind blew up and the whole surface shattered and cut into a million shining bits, exposing the jelly insides of the water within, cobalt, silken.

So much water. Miles of it under you, washing through underwater caves, one shelf of water tipping over into another, vast secret lakes, a whole world of water beneath, prehistoric. It was hundreds of miles of past and future washing through itself in endless, moonless tides. Water, water, all water. Of course our mark upon it, our frail kicking... Of course it could have been no more than leaves scattered across the surface. So much water, you can't change it. You can imagine other things you could have done, if you want, rack over in your mind details, events, names of people and their ages... But does any of this give you more than what you started out with?

The water has them, those people you pretend were your life. It has you. It's water's pulse beating in your wrist now. You know it too. The lake, she's your lovely body now, with all her openings. Close your eyes, she's still there. Some days the surface of water is pulled over like satin, others it's rumpled and bony. There's your memory. Pure images of tide and depth and the color of the water ...These are things you can still use. Who you were, who you are now, your people...They're drowned in her. All the rest is water.

I remember how, long ago, my little brother and I used to go out into the summer rain. We were disappearing or returning, I don't know. We were going into water. There at the lake, rain was so gentle. It was a drift, a veil of gray and silver, like the sails of ghost ships, gauzy. There was cloud in the rain too, white mists lifting off the lake so water tended into the air like it lived there. Slowly it stained, there was no violence to it, no individual drops, it was melting rain. The beach sunk into a deeper color, and it happened so gradually that at first you could see no change at all. Then you would press on the sand with your toes and find it warm, slatey. The powder of it had condensed with moisture, you could squeeze it, shape it into castles and islands and towers. Whole cities we could leave molded on the beach and all the time as we worked the rain softened them, merged into vague dream shapes, hills.

Up behind the beach rain smoothed the dry grass down and the fields of lupins were shiny, their yellow like wet paint against the pale gray.

In rain we could take off our clothes and walk down the beach and into the lake in one continuous gliding movement. There was no telling where land ended, waves began. Sand and water dissolved into each other, blotted in mist. Nothing else existed on those days except two children. Watch them. Two with the whole beach to themselves, the whiteness of cloud and water swirling at their feet as they dance, round and around, round and around...With each turn becoming smaller, further away, smaller and smaller in the distance until you can't see them at all.

Knight-Errant

No, I said *badinage*, not *bandage*,
Protective clothing for the psyche,
Not the dressing of bloodied tissue.
Behind my small talk can be heard
A constant jingling of the plates
That cover my vulnerability,
Each placed to parry or disarm
Projectiles like the sharpened word.

No, those are not the marks of rust.
This armor is meant to be lived in,
With its chinks and seams and weak points,
Which some days let in more than air.
I fancy myself on a charger.
Watch me prancing across the courtyard,
Coconut shells on cobbles, sunbeams
Gilding my greaves and savoir faire.

Getting out will be something else.
I seem to have grown into this panoply
Which cannot be molted like plumage
Or left as one might leave a smart hotel.
I reckon to be hoisted by sheerlegs
Or, as in a forceps delivery,
Be drawn out head first, pale and curling,
A shrimp extracted from its shell.

Up and Down

Today I caught sight of the griffon vultures
Making for the land bridge and Africa—
A cue for me to assemble
And drive our sheep, crying and tinkling,
Down from the mile-high summer pastures
To the folds and knives of the valley.

I spend weeks up here on my own
Either side of the longest day,
My mind as empty as an airship.
The dogs run around and do the work
Or flop down on ledges of rock,
Watching for wanderers.

In my country we eat peas with a spoon,
We do not queue for buses, and the demand
For Western diseases of affluence
Far exceeds the supply.
The lammergeiers drop our bones
Out of the blue, hungry for marrow.

Stuck with half-exile and geology,
I have lost the knack of conversation.
Winters in the town are full of awkwardness,
Silence over backgammon
And jokes that pass me by
Screaming like swifts.

Last year in a smoky room I learned
That a fisherman on a visit
Had taken away my girl;
And the old man in the corner,
Curved like a sickle,
Was said to have minded flocks in the mountains.

Interesting Times

When the pestilence had left Newcastle
We sent in the prisoners of war
As an advance guard to clear the rats
And burn their carcasses on waste land
Between the town and the hills to the north.
And to these dry hills we then despatched
The prisoners, giving them their freedom.
It is not known how many survived
Or what caused the deaths of those who perished.

The burial of our own dead we left
To the old people, arguing fairly
That they had an abundance of memories
And must possess a kind of immunity
To have lived so gradely and so long.
But after the carting and interment
In mass graves, they were required to camp
For six weeks outside the eastern gate.
We were pleased to see how many returned.

The rest of us, except for the wounded,
Small children and women at full term,
Sweated for days on the muddy bankside,
Humping up full buckets from the river
To sluice the filth out of the buildings.
Months later we might still catch the stench.
Few if any sexual relationships
Were brokered or resumed in this period,
But there was a brisk market in commodities.

Electricity has become a legend,
A concept the young ones cannot grasp.
And sometimes we forget to boil the water
Or lack the fuel with which to do so,
Having consumed it in the imperative
To forge new weapons and new defenses
From scrap metals of the past regime.
These we render down, though there are alloys
Beyond our ability to melt.

Elsewhere the future may be in progress,
While here traffic makes its way on foot,
Porterage being a sort of livelihood.
The insects having returned to office
With their doctrinaire policies, losing
Is what we appear to be condemned to.
Laws, so-called, are vested in hard hands,
But we pass our nights in fear of pilferers
And our leisure at knuckle-bones and hazard.

Richard

Prince

Adult

Comedy

Action

Drama

Richard Prince

Adult Comedy Action Drama

Ein Künstlerbuch

SCALO

BLOCKBUSTER VIDEO

MEMBERSHIP CARD ®

56-0029   VIDEO EXPRESS   № 8606
Home Entertainment Centers Inc.
20 Mall
Guilderland, NY 12084

MEMBERSHIP CARD

THIS IS TO CERTIFY THAT

Richard Prince

ss

IS A MEMBER IN GOOD STANDING

FROM _____ TO 7/3

NSFERABLE   AUTHORIZED SIGNATURE

ST★RDUST *Video*

WATER MILL SQUARE
MONTAUK HIGHWAY
WATER MILL, NEW YORK 11976
516-726-5115

EO CLUB
SHIP AGREEMENT

#8606
at Guilderland

SELECTION

ME   Prince Richard.

HORIZED BY   Billy   EXPIRY

E READ AND AGREE TO ABIDE BY THE TERMS AND CONDITIONS ON REVERSE.

ED X _____ DATE 11/3/91

M-187515

Price Chopper SUPERMARKETS

#28

STORE NO.

12/26/91
DATE ISSUED

Richard Prince
NAME

SIGNATURE

INSTANT
MEMBERSHIP
CARD
3221895
CARD NO.

P Pre
AUTHORIZED BY

FAMILY VIDEO PLUS
BRYANTS COUNTRY SQUARE
GREENVILLE, N.Y. 12083
518-966-5115

797-3567

Richard Prince

ne

3079
_____ Date _____ Effective

Video Express
20 Mall
Guilderland, NY
456-0029

Initials

10

Member No.
8606

Movie Punch Card
Good for Ten Movie Rentals

☆ ☆ ☆ ☆

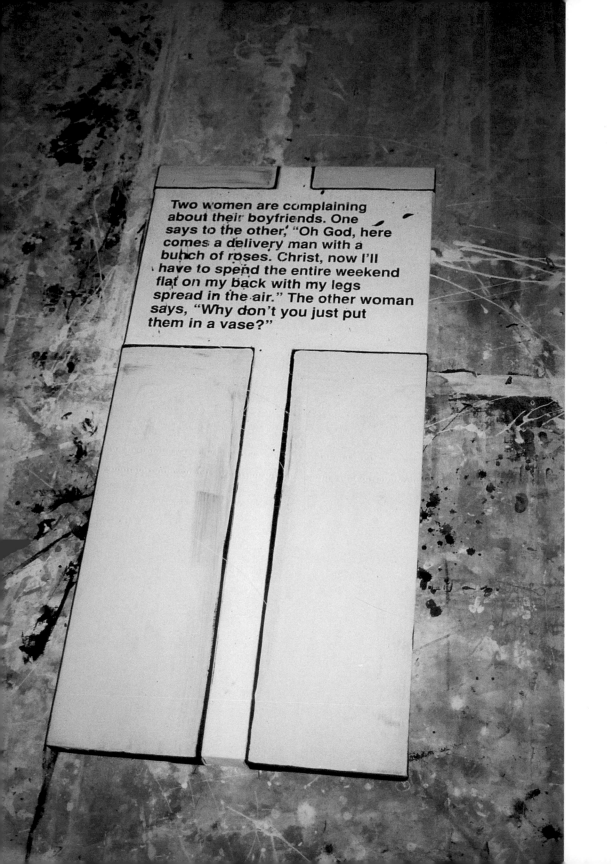

Two women are complaining about their boyfriends. One says to the other, "Oh God, here comes a delivery man with a bunch of roses. Christ, now I'll have to spend the entire weekend flat on my back with my legs spread in the air." The other woman says, "Why don't you just put them in a vase?"

A wife tells her husband he's the world's biggest schmuck. "In fact," she says, "if they had a contest for schmucks, you'd come in second." "Why second?" he asks. Says the wife, "Because you're a schmuck!"

13x41

Richard Prince jokes   galley 1

My parents kept me in a closet for years. Until I was fifteen I thought I was a suit.

One day a Greek insulted a Spaniard. The next morning, the Germans declared war!

Hey Thanks very much.

Kelp

After the week of storms
the shore was gone.
A wrack of stinking strands
had pressed up onto the beach.

Yellow-brown the tangled roots,

the thousand names of kelp,

abandoned to mulch, once funneled up
from submarine forests,
deeper than memory,
placid waters of imagining.

Rock   sea   silence   wash;

the salt-tongue dragging, dragging.

White birds picked at it.
Starfish crept under it.
Our own feet churned
across its shining vocabulary.

All summer it rotted.
Its stash of beauty decayed.
No one came to dredge and stack it,
to burn it to a white hot ash.

Artists' Sessions at Studio 35, New York, April 21, 22, 23, 1950

Adolph Gottlieb
Hans Hofmann
Alfred H. Barr, Jr.
Robert Motherwell
Richard Lippold
Willem de Kooning

Peter Grippe
Jimmy Ernst
Norman Lewis
Seymour Lipton

Ibram Lassaw
James Brooks
Ad Reinhardt
Richard Pousette-Dart

Jimmy Ernst
Norman Lewis
Seymour Lipton
Barnett Newman

David Hare (obscured)
Hedda Sterne
Robert Goodnough
Janice Biala
Bradley Walker Tomlin
Herbert Ferber

James Brooks
Ad Reinhardt
Richard Pousette-Dart
Louise Bourgeois

Art World Details: Journal Excerpts

1 November 1955. To Jackson Pollock: "I saw a movie you'd like—*Rebel Without a Cause.* The story's heavily psychiatric, but Dean's performance is terrific."

"I'm not involved with movies."

"You'd like this. It's as good as *The Wild One.*"

"What do they know about being wild? I'm wild. There's wildness in me. There's wildness in my hands."

14 January 1956. Clyfford Still: "Don't think I'm a bitter old man. I had San Francisco in the palm of my hand. . . . I don't care about the audience, I want to put the emphasis back on the artist. The painting is an act, a part of the artist's life. I won't let it become an object. I won't let the Museum of Modern Art put it through the meat grinder. They're afraid of anything that's alive. They want scalps for their walls."

15 January 1956. Robert Rauschenberg: "The aura of Pollock got ahead of him."

5 February 1956. Last week Morty [Feldman] called from a booth to say that he had the phone in his apartment turned off so he can work and also that he had sent Cynthia to her parents'. But still

B.H. Friedman and Jackson Pollock at Eddie Condon's, May 14, 1954

he can't work. When I told him that Musa and Philip [Guston] were at our place, he said he'd come right over. I hadn't realized that having the phone turned off is a pattern of Philip's also and that, among the conventions of Morty's and Philip's very close friendship, is each of them always thinking that the dead phone is directed at him personally. So, first Morty had to reassure Philip that Philip had done nothing to offend him. Only then did I feel free to suggest that perhaps each of them turns off the phone not because he's afraid that people *will* call but that they won't.

6 February 1956. Saul Steinberg at Betty and Bob Motherwell's: "I don't read palms. Anyone can read palms. I read feet. Palms tell you about the future. Feet tell you about the past. I don't care about tomorrow. I care about yesterday."

13 August 1956. Just learned that Jackson died in a car crash Saturday night. Ruth [Kligman] badly hurt. Friend of hers also died. I can't help thinking that Abby and I might have been killed two weekends earlier under similar circumstances.

17 January 1957. Sam Hunter: "Greenberg says Smith is the best sculptor of his time."

Bob Motherwell: "Best is too general. He's the best David Smith of his time."

20 April 1957. Franz Kline: "For forty-seven years I gave them their reality and they didn't understand it. Now I give them my reality and they think they understand it."

24 April 1957. Evening with Lee [Krasner] and Sidney Janis repricing Pollocks for the Whitney Museum's consideration. The confusion between economic symbolism (i.e. market price) and value. Lee's fear that the price will affect the true value of Jackson's work because the price is an acceptance of *other people's values.* At the same time her refusal to think in terms of a current market, only a future market. Oscar Wilde comes full circle: knowing the value of everything and the price of nothing. Pollock must now, after he is dead, become an economic success.

Jackson Pollock, *Untitled,* c. 1943

25 May 1957. The Picasso opening at MoMA was show biz. Gala. A careful mixture of the wealthy, the talented, the attractive. Picasso, hanging on the walls and placed on pedestals, was the single dominant symbol of all three qualities, and he remained remote, unique, difficult to see. I made the effort, but the social spectacle in the background could not be ignored: [Alfred] Barr, wearing the paper tie painted and sent by Picasso *"pour le vernissage"*; the Spanish guitarists; the younger painters like Joan Mitchell and Mike Goldberg and Grace Hartigan completely potted and "bored by Picasso." Joan described the show as "a drag," but the drag was strong as an undertow. Picasso is still, at seventy-five, the supreme threat, and the inventor of that most challenging of conventions, the continuously new style. Until Picasso no one expected an artist's style to change, but only to mature. Now the world asks, "What's new?"

16 June 1957. Tonight on the television program *$64,000 Challenge* Larry Rivers and the "art expert" jockey Billy Pierson tied, each receiving $32,000. An important date in the history of contemporary art!

31 August 1957. East Hampton is becoming an insane asylum. One becomes involved with a crowd that is both too inbred and too large—exactly what one tries to escape from in the city.

20 November 1957. Sultry silent Marisol spoke at her opening, "The people are too strong for my work." But at Esteban Vicente's opening, after not saying a word when they were introduced, he asked, "Don't you like my work?"
    M: "No-ooo."
    E.V.: (taken aback) "What do you do?"
    M: "Paint."
    E.V.: (cuttingly) "Who do you paint like?"
    M: (after long pause) "You-ooo."

9 January 1958. The sadness last night of going through Bob Motherwell's library, being offered books for 50¢ a piece that he'd spent his lifetime collecting—the record of his life, of his involvements with philosophy, French literature, Surrealism. I understand his need to unload, his desire to travel light, but for him, as for me, it's a fantasy. Some of us will always travel heavy, will always accumulate possessions, will seek or invent complications, even if there are none.

His nostalgia for Surrealism was moving too: the yearning for intellectual brilliance and exchange combined with the ability to see innocently, the yearning for a visit to a bookshop with Magritte. . . . And yet his having almost forgotten the dictatorial aspects of the Surrealist world, the cruelty, the insensitivity, the nightmare of life-as-a-game when this principle is applied to human relations.

25 January 1958. It's 5 a.m. Bob's birthday party is over. He said, as he's said several times before, that I'm an aristocrat. I smiled, as I've smiled several times before, unbelievingly. He said, "I mean that whenever there's a check to pay, you pay it, at precisely the right moment and as gently as possible, but whenever anyone puts pressure on you to buy something, you refuse."

24 May 1958. Bob was right when he referred to his generation of American painters as Abstract Surrealists—right not only in thus regarding himself, but also Newman, Still, Pollock, Rothko, Gottlieb. . . . Now the issue is suppressed and Barney is accused of Constructivism or Neoplasticism. Barney's "defenders," like Clem [Greenberg], confuse things more by asserting that there is nothing programmatic about his work, as though a program in itself were pejorative. Barney has one: it's to destroy the painting surface, to destroy interest in it for its own sake, to allow color (without surface interest) to become a statement. The statement is limited; the gesture is large.

25 July 1958. Ab tells me that Lee has been "dismissed" by her analyst. In this case, since the analyst is so immature, dismissal means that he has gotten as much help from her as he can.

8 August 1958. What I think Barney said for the past hour or so on the phone: "Everything about this 103rd Street apartment is perfect, except the location. It's a little frightening when we go out at night. The trouble is thugs never ask what you do, or I'd tell

Left to right: (front) Lee Krasner, Abby Friedman, Annalee Newman, Barnett Newman, (back) B.H. Friedman, Sheridan Lord

them I live by my wits, too. They see a guy who's dressed well and they assume he's rich. They don't recognize style, as such. If they rob you or hurt you or kill you, it's always a case of mistaken identity."

17 January 1959. Barney remarked, "I was one of the few artists who matured in the Thirties who was never attracted to communism." Harold Rosenberg's name came up, and Barney said, "It's ridiculous to talk about that guy as a revolutionary, to hear him talk about himself as one. He was involved with velvet—the free fuck, the free ride, the free rations. They were all involved with velvet."

22 February 1959. Jon [Schueler]'s party at June Lathrop's Friday night for the troupe of the Ballets Africaines failed when people became involved with the idea of "intercultural relations." For example, a middle-aged lady asked one of the troupe: *"De quelle tribe êtes-vous?"*

The dancer replied: *"Je suis pygmée."*

16 May 1959. Helen [Frankenthaler] calling her psychiatrist about whether or not to fire her butler.

18 July 1959 (East Hampton). Jack Kerouac, arriving at Lee's surrounded by an entourage: "I thought this was an open party."

Lee: "It's not *that* open."

19 March 1960. At the Bultmans' dancing party Franz Kline told a story about a couple whose sixteen-year-old son was "doing Klines."

"Everything's reversed," Franz continued. "They used to say that Matisses looked like children's drawings.... Now they say children's drawings look like Klines."

7 June 1960. Barney: "I hate official artists' wives. I hate their attitude—you make the paintings, and I'll take care of the career."

27 November 1960 (At the Sculls' in Great Neck). Ethel and Bob have a beautiful art collection in an ugly house, large and new. It's difficult to understand how the same house can contain a dozen or more Klines, half a dozen de Koonings, etc. and not a single attractive ashtray.

Rauschenberg is wearing a dandy's suit, with lapels about the width of piping, a double-breasted vest, and pants which someone describes as so tight that he doesn't have to take them off when the doctor says, "Cough!" I ask who his tailor is and he says Donard, between 13th and 14th Street on Broadway, five flights up. This is the essence of Rauschenberg's style, finding beauty in unlikely places.

De Kooning is well decked out in one of twelve suits he got from "the best tailor in Rome." Kline is elegantly dressed in a dark suit. The two of them, despite their humble backgrounds, emerge in almost any crowd, certainly in this one, as a pair of natural aristocrats. Johns is wearing an ordinary dark suit but a Christmassy red-and-silver tie which is both a parody and an abstraction.

I encourage talk about clothes, since I have a vague idea of writing a book about contemporary dandyism. The artists are understandably delighted with their newfound ability to *afford* things. They are self-conscious in an unapologetic way, a contrast to the way of the Fifties.

19 February 1961. The evening of St. Valentine's the Motherwells drove us to La Crémaillère in their Bentley. Three of us had pheasant or venison *à la maison.* After dinner we returned slowly to New York through heavy fog. Then a brief visit to Helen's new spacious studio. And then, just before they delivered us home, Helen gave Abby and me little presents: two coins. Abby's is a half-dollar-size aluminum disc with the center pressed out in the shape of a star, like those on which children stamp their names. This one says: STOP ABSTRACT EXPRESSIONISM. My coin is smaller, about the size of a quarter. One side says ACCEPTED and shows a little boy playing baseball. The other side says REJECTED and the boy's head is bowed. Ever since Helen gave me this coin I've wanted to flip it, to find out what's happening to my novel at Putnam's. Friday the manuscript arrived in the mail, REJECTED. I flip the coin now. Too late, it comes up ACCEPTED.

2 September 1961. I tell Alfonso [Ossorio] that his work is heading toward the ultimate Crucifixion: a human body fixed in polyvinyl acetate.

"If I did that," he replies, "I'd use the head of Frankenthaler and the body of Motherwell. But what I really want to do is the Resurrection."

23 December 1961. Reinhardt: "Guston's always saying, 'I knew Pollock when he was nothing.' I knew Guston when he was something."

7 March 1962. Barney [Newman]: "Los Angeles is like Brooklyn and East Hampton pushed together with no Manhattan in between."

25 October 1962. Today Harold Rosenberg appeared for the first time as author of the art column in *The New Yorker.* There was an argument, some ten years ago, between him and Berton Rouché when Rosenberg asked how Rouché could work for such a "slick" publication. Once again, things come full circle.

23 December 1962 (Turtle Bay Gardens). At breakfast Abby is still hung over from last night's party at Anita Ellis's. (I couldn't go because of flu.) Abby returned at about three a.m. with Frank O'Hara. I heard them, called on the intercom, and they came up to the bedroom for a nightcap. It lasted about two hours. At first Frank was very gentle and funny about rescuing Abby from "all those people on the make," but after a while he began attacking the art in our bedroom while at the same time selling Mike Goldberg and Norman Bluhm.

Everything must be attacked that isn't part of Frank's camp. For example, it's not enough for him to say Kline is a good painter, he's got to make him "better than Miró."

Franz Kline, *Jackson*, c. 1954–56.

30 January 1963. Frank said that Bonnie [Golightly] had come over to him at a party, grabbed him around the waist, and lifted him into the air. "I just felt like picking up a poet," she said.

Later Frank left Bonnie to get a drink, saying, "There's another poet." He pointed at Kenneth Koch. "Pick him up."

"I don't know if I can. I've never read his poems."

25 July 1964 (Provincetown). Helen: "I'm the best woman painter in America and what am I doing? Running two houses here and one in New York, entertaining, taking care of children, doing everything but paint."

10 January 1965. When Lee and Jackson moved to East Hampton, Bob Motherwell was already there considering a piece of property across the road. One night he was at their place and, after many drinks, said, "I'm going to be the best-known artist in America."

Lee said, "I'd be very lucky to live opposite the best-known artist in America and be married to the best."

13 October 1965. Howard Kanovitz mentioned a night in the early Fifties at the Cedar Tavern. Pollock, de Kooning, Kline, and others were there. Howie was standing near the entrance when two tourists came in. They looked around quickly and one said to the other: "This is the place where the painters are supposed to come, but there's no one here tonight."

6 December 1965. Jon Schueler tells me about the sad bad shape de Kooning is in: he's drinking heavily and hasn't painted for several months. On the main wall of the studio he has been building and rebuilding there are two small drawings and, off to the side, many doors are stacked, intended to be used as panels—in short, signs of preparation but virtually no completed work. Jon continues, "There's a common expression among painters: 'studio-building.' That means activity we manufacture when we're not working."

8 January 1966. Lee is thinking about an apartment in the city. Meanwhile, she's in a room at the Elysée Hotel surrounded by separate piles of catalogues, announcements, Christmas cards (unacknowledged), correspondence (unanswered), books (unopened or with place-markers near the beginning), real estate brokers' business cards, three different address books...all stacked, arranged, and rearranged, seemingly according to some system of priority. Finally her highest priority becomes clear: total inertia. She may be in this room forever, with only the company of its television set (always on).

24 January 1966. Dali's entertainment at Van Wolf's: the North African musicians, the dancing girls, the entourage of models, the cheetah, the trainer. Dali himself as always in costume: the gold lamé tie, the brocaded vest, the gold-handled cane which he waves around phallically. He looks exhausted. He has become one of his own props. He leaves promptly at midnight as though fearful that if he stayed longer he might turn into—Dali.

3 March 1966. Lee: "Motherwell said somewhere that after a time he stopped painting with just his hand and wrist and began using his arm. He discovered his arm! He moved up from the wrist to the shoulder. But it still hasn't occurred to him that you can paint with your whole body, that that's what American painting is all about."

8 June 1966. I was shocked to read my piece on Helen Frankenthaler in the June *ARTnews*, shocked not only by deletions but by changes in content precisely where I had already compromised with her after suggesting that the article might be assigned to someone else rather than risk our friendship. Hoping that she herself had not made these changes, I wrote a letter to Tom Hess [editor of *ARTnews*]. He called today to tell me he couldn't say anything but that I could read between the lines. I "read." I understood that Helen had chosen careerism over friendship.

20 July 1966. Fritz Bultman reminiscing about Hofmann's use of the English language: "He once said to a model, 'I'd like to screw you on the floor.' He meant that her pose was so beautiful he wanted to fix her there to the floor, ready for the next time he painted. . . . When an author sent him a book, he wrote that he was anxious to *overlook* it."

27 July 1966. Monday night Helen called with the news of Frank O'Hara's accident and again, later, of his death. Still later Howie called. He had heard from Larry. Each phone call, each new detail, each "fact"—until the final fact—compounded the gratuitous, becoming a drama of the absurd.

I slept fitfully, thinking of Frank's "accident" and Jackson's. This morning I awoke before six and reread a long poem of Frank's, the only one I have here in Provincetown: *Biotherm.* I hope if Bill Berkson, to whom the poem is dedicated, delivers a eulogy he will quote this line: "I don't think I want to win anything I think I want to die unadorned"—a line from which most of the art world could learn.

12 February 1967. Jim Dine: "I've never prostituted myself, my work."

Me: "But, in a sense, doesn't every artist sell his love?"

Jim: "No, an art prostitute is one who does work he doesn't love—for example, someone who doesn't like doing portraits but accepts commissions to do them."

Thus as the night lengthened, we redefined prostitution, not as selling love but as assuming unnatural positions.

7 April 1967 (Ithaca). Party after Jim's opening and John Ashbery's reading. Kitchen table becomes a mountainous assemblage of empty bottles, beer cans, cartons, wrappings, cigarette butts, bits of food, utensils.... Someone picks up a bottle cap on the table and someone else says, "Put it back. You'll destroy the whole thing. It's so beautiful." A moment later someone asks for a corkscrew. Jim begins looking for it, deliberately shoving around the piles of stuff on the table. Garbage spills on the floor. Bottles break. Beer cans clatter. Spider's rock band plays on in the background. There's no corkscrew, but there's a new composition on the table.

9 October 1969. After not seeing Alfonso in several years, Jean Dubuffet greets him (in French): "Are you happy?"
   "Reasonably."
   "Today?"
   "Yes."
   "For a week?"
   "Yes."
   "A month?"
   "Yes."
   "That's a long time. You're more than reasonably happy—you're unreasonably happy."
   I urge Dubuffet to see the Oldenburg show at the Modern and, to persuade him, I mention that Oldenburg's early work is influenced by him and also that in one work Oldenburg incorporates Dubuffet's name along with Céline's.
   Dubuffet smiles, showing the large amount of gold in his teeth. "I like that, when an artist advertises his sources. I will write a note to Oldenburg."
   "But you won't go to the museum?"
   "No, that would be like the devil passing through the gates of a church."

5 July 1970. My brother Sandy called from East Hampton to say that Barney Newman had died. In the *New York Times* obituary much was inaccurate, especially describing him as a "leader of the shaped-canvas movement."

26 October 1972. Dubuffet described trying to phone from the Fifth Avenue hotel to his wife in Paris: "They don't know my name. They make me spell it: D as in Düsseldorf. U as in Ursula. B as in Biafra. U as in Ursula *encore.* F—F was very hard—thoughts ran through my mind. F as in Farango. F *encore.* E as in Elysia. T as in Trinity."

At Chase Manhattan Plaza, we examined his forty-foot sculpture of stylized trees. "I have learned a lot from this commission," he said. "Next time I will raise the black lines, make them sculptural. In my house outside Paris, I have a garden of my trees, surrounded by high walls. Absolutely private. Only for my pleasure. And that of a few friends *perhaps.*"

His blue-gray eyes brightened in his shaved head, like two small bulbs within a large bulb. He is a young man in his seventies.

14 July 1978. Shocked by Tom Hess's death, a day after Harold Rosenberg's, I immediately thought of the pending acquisition of Alfonso's sculpture by the Metropolitan and also wondered who would replace Tom at the museum and Harold at *The New Yorker.* On the phone I said something to Alfonso about Clem Greenberg being next, then said I'd better pray to be forgiven. Alfonso told me not to worry, that everyone in East Hampton has been saying the same thing.

1 February 1987. Ab tells Jon that MoMA was very crowded.

Jon: "We used to complain that the philistines didn't come to our shows. Now we complain that they do."

The Black Book

Was the voice, which Galip Jelal imagined belonging to someone with a white collar, worn jacket, and a phantom face, forming these sentences impromptu by virtue of an overactive memory, or was it reading them off a prompter? Galip thought it over. The voice took Galip's silence as a sign and gave a victorious laugh. Sharing the ends of the same phone cable, which went by way of who knew what underground passages and below what hills teeming with Ottoman skulls and Byzantine coins, clinging like black ivy to the walls of old apartment buildings where the plaster was falling off, strung tight like clotheslines between rusty poles and along plane and chestnut trees, he whispered as if confiding a secret with the brotherly love instilled by sharing an umbilical cord attached to the same mother: he had much love for Jelal; he had much respect for Jelal; he had much knowledge of Jelal. Jelal didn't have any doubt about any of this anymore, did he?

"I wouldn't know," Galip said.

"In that case, let's get rid of these black telephones between us," said the voice. Because the bell on the phone which sometimes rang on its own accord alarmed rather than alerted; because the pitch-black receiver was heavy as a little dumbbell, and when dialed, it grumbled with the squeaky melody of the old turnstiles at the Karaköy-Kadiköy ferryboat dock; because sometimes it connected with numbers at random rather than the numbers dialed. "Get it, Mr. Jelal? Give me your address and I'll be right over."

Galip hesitated at first, like a teacher struck dumb by the wonders performed by a wonder student, and then—astonished that the man's garden of memory seemed to have no bounds, astonished as well by the flowers that bloomed in the garden of his own memory, and aware of the trap he was gradually falling into—he asked: "What about nylon stockings?"

"In a piece you wrote in 1958, two years after the time when you were obliged to publish your column not under your own name but under some hapless pseudonyms you came up with, on a hot summer day when you were stressed out with work and loneliness, watching a movie which was halfway through in a Beyoğlu movie theater (the Rüya) where you took refuge from the noonday sun, you wrote that you were startled by a sound you heard nearby, through the laughter of Chicago gangsters dubbed into Turkish by pitiful Beyoğlu dubbers, the report of machine guns, and the crash of bottles and glass: somewhere not too far off the long fingernails of a woman were scratching her legs through her nylons. When the first feature was over and the house lights went on, you saw, sitting two rows in front of you, a beautiful stylish mother and her well-behaved eleven-year-old son talking to each other like chums. For a long while you observed their camaraderie, how they carefully listened to each other. In another piece two years later, you'd write that, watching the second feature, you were not listening to the clash of steel blades and storms on the high seas that roared out of the sound system but to the buzz produced by the restless hand with long fingernails traveling on legs that would feed Istanbul's mosquitoes on summer nights, and that your mind was not on the pirates' dirty deals on the screen, but on the friendship between the mother and son. As you revealed in a column you wrote twelve years after that, your publisher had scolded you soon after the publication of the piece with the nylons: Had you no idea that it was dangerous, a very dangerous practice, to focus on the sexuality of a wife and mother? That the Turkish reader would not tolerate it? And that if you wished to survive as a columnist, you had to be careful with what you said about married women as well as your writing style?"

"On style? Make it brief, please."

"For you, style was life. Style, for you, was voice. Style was your thoughts. Style was your real persona you created within it, but this was not one, not two, but three personas...."

"These are?"

"The first voice is what you call "my simple persona": the voice that you reveal to anyone, the one with which you sit down at family dinners and gossip through billows of smoke after dinner. You owe this persona the details of your everyday life. The second voice belongs to the person you wish to be: a mask that you appropriated from admirable personages who, having found no peace in this world, live in another and are suffused with its mystery. You'd written that you would have holed up in a corner, unable to face life, waiting for death like many an unhappy person if it hadn't been for your habit of whispering with this 'hero' whom you initially wanted to imitate and then become, if it hadn't been for your habit of repeating, like a senile person reciting the refrains stuck in his mind, the acrostics, the puzzles, parodies, and banter that this hero whispered in your ear. I was in tears reading it. What took you—and me, naturally—into realms unavailable to the first two personas you call 'the objective and subjective styles' was the third voice: the dark persona, the dark style! I know even better than you what it was that you wrote on nights when you were too unhappy to be satisfied with imitation and masks; but you know better what it was that you perpetrated, brother mine! We're meant to understand each other, find one another, and put on disguises together; give me your address."

"Addresses?"

"Cities are composed of addresses, addresses of letters, just as faces of letters. On Monday, October 12, 1963, you described Kurtuluş, called Tatavla in the old days, an Armenian quarter, as one of your most beloved spots in Istanbul. I read it with pleasure."

"Reading?"

"On one occasion, in February of 1962, should you require a date, during the tense days when you were preparing for a military coup that would save the nation from poverty, on one of the dark streets in Beyoğlu, you'd seen a gilt-framed large mirror—being carried, goodness knows for what strange reason, from one nightclub where belly dancers and jugglers operate to another—which had first cracked, perhaps due to the cold, and then had burst into smithereens right before your eyes; that's when you'd realized it wasn't for nothing that the word in our language for the stuff that turns glass into mirror is the same as the word for 'secret.' After divulging this moment of insight in one of your columns, you'd said this: Reading is looking in the mirror; those who know the 'secret' behind the glass manage to go through the looking-glass; and those who have no knowledge of letters will find nothing more in the world than their own dull faces."

"What's the secret?"

"I'm the only one besides you who knows the secret. You know very well it's not something that can be discussed over the phone. Give me your address."

"What's the secret?"

"Don't you realize a reader has to devote his whole life to you to get to the secret? That's what I've done. Shaking with cold in unheated state libraries, an overcoat on my back, hat on my head, and woolen gloves on my hands, I've read everything I suspected you might've written, the stuff you knocked off when you didn't publish under your own name, the serials you wrote passing for someone else, the puzzles, the portraits, the politically and emotionally charged interviews, just to figure out what the secret might be. Given that you have produced without fail eight pages a day on the average, in thirty-some years your output would be a hundred thousand pages, or three hundred volumes, each three-hundred-thirty-three pages. This nation ought to erect your statue just for that!"

"Yours too, for having read it all," Galip said. "What about statues?"

"On one of my Anatolian trips, in a small town the name of which I've forgotten, I was waiting in the town square park until it was time for my bus when a youngish person sat beside me and we began to talk. We started by mentioning the statue of Atatürk pointing at the bus terminal as if the only viable thing to do in this pitiful town was to leave it. Then, at my instigation, we talked about a column of yours on the subject of Atatürk statues which number over ten thousand throughout our country. You'd written that on the day of the apocalypse, when lightning and lightning bolts tore through the dark sky and quakes moved the firmament, all those terrifying Atatürk statues would come to life. According to what you wrote, some of the statues wearing pigeon droppings and European garb, some in the field marshal's uniform and decorations, some riding rearing stallions with large male organs, some in top hats and phantom-like capes, they would all start moving slowly in place; then they would get down from their bases which are covered with flowers and wreaths, and around which dusty old buses and horse carts have circled for years, and where soldiers whose uniforms smell of sweat and high-school girls whose uniforms smell of mothballs have gathered to sing the national anthem, and all these statues would vanish into the dark. The obsessive young man had read the piece where you described the night of the apocalypse when the ground quaked and the sky was rent, how our poor citizens listening to the roar outside through their closed windows would hearken with abject fear to the sounds of bronze and marble boots and hooves on the slum sidewalks, and the young man had become so overwhelmed that he had immediately written you a letter impatiently inquiring when the day of the apocalypse would come. If what he said was true, then you'd sent him a short answer asking him for a document-size photo; and after you got it, you'd given him the secret 'omen of the impending Day.' Don't get me wrong, the secret you gave the young man was not 'The Secret.' Disappointed after waiting for years at the park where the pool had gone dry and the grass had become patchy, the young man had divulged to me your secret that must have been, perforce, personal. You'd explained to him the secondary meanings of some letters and told him to consider a sentence he'd someday run across in your writing as a sign. Reading that sentence, our young man would decipher the encoded column and get to work."

"What was the sentence?"

"'My entire life was full of these sorts of horrible memories.' There, that was the sentence. I can't figure out if he'd made it up or if you'd actually written it to him, but the coincidence is that, these days when you complain that your memory has been stunted or even completely erased, I've read this sentence, as well as others, in an old piece that's recently been rerun. Give me your address and I'll give you an instant explanation of what it means."

"What about other sentences?"

"Give me your address! Give it. I happen to know that you aren't curious about any other sentences or stories. You've given up on this country so thoroughly that you're not curious about anything. Your screws are getting loose from loneliness in that rat's nest where you're hiding out hatefully, without friends, comrades, anybody.... Give me your address so that I can tell you in just which secondhand bookstore you might find students from the Religious High School who trade your autographed pictures, and wrestling umpires who fancy young boys. Give me your address so I can show you the etchings depicting eighteen Ottoman sultans who had assignations in secret places around Istanbul with their own harem wives whom they had masquerading as European whores. Did you know that in high-class haberdasheries and whorehouses in Paris this disease which requires wearing lots of dressy clothes and jewelry is called 'the Turk's disease'? Did you know of the etching that shows Mahmut the Second, who copulated in disguise on some dark street in Istanbul wearing on his naked legs the boots Napoleon wore on his campaign to Egypt? And that his favorite wife, Bezm-i Alem, the Queen Mother—that is, the grandmother of the prince whose story you like so much and the godmother of an Ottoman ship—is shown in the same picture nonchalantly wearing a diamond and ruby cross?"

"What about crosses?" Galip said with some sort of joy, aware that he was getting some pleasure in life for the first time since his wife left him six days and four hours ago.

"I know it was no coincidence that under your January 18, 1958 column, right below your lines harping on Egyptian geometry, Arab algebra, and Syriac Neoplatonism in order to prove that the cross as a form was the opposite of the crescent—its repudiation and negation—appeared the news concerning the marriage of Edward G. Robinson, whom I really love as the 'cigar-chomping tough guy of the cinema and the stage,' to the New York clothes designer Jane Adler, showing a photograph of the newlyweds under the shadow of a crucifix. Give me your address. A week later, you'd proposed that instilling a phobia for the cross and zealotry for the crescent in our children resulted in stunting them into adults incapable of deciphering Hollywood's magical faces, leading them to sexual disorientation such as imagining all moonfaced women to be either mothers or aunts; and in order to prove your point, you'd claimed that if state boarding schools for the poor were to be raided on the nights after the kids studied the Crusades in history class, hundreds of them would be discovered having peed in their beds. These are just bits and pieces; give me your address, and I'll bring you all the stories about crosses that you want, all the stuff I came across in provincial newspapers, scratching around in libraries for your work. 'Having escaped the gallows when the oiled noose around his neck snapped, a convict tells about the crosses he saw on his short trip to Hell, upon returning from the realm of the dead.' *The Erciyaş Post*, Kayseri, 1962. 'Our edi.or-in-chief has wired .he Presiden., poin.ing ou. .ha. using .he period ins.ead of .he obviously cross-shaped le..er is more in keeping wi.h .urkish cul.ure.' *Green Konya*, Konya, 1951. If you give me your address I'll rush you many more....I'm not suggesting that these are material for your writing; I know that you hate columnists who regard life as grist for the mill. I can bring the stuff that sits in boxes in front of me right over; we'd read it together, laughing and weeping. Come on, give me the address, I'll bring you stories serialized in İskenderun papers about local men who could only stop stuttering when they were telling hookers at nightclubs how much they hated their fathers. Give me your address and I'll bring you love and death predictions made by a waiter who was not only illiterate, he couldn't even speak proper Turkish, let alone Persian, but who could recite Omar Khayyam's undiscovered poems on account of their souls being twins; give me your address. I'll bring you the dreams of a journalist-printer from Bayburt who, upon discovering that he was losing his memory, serialized on the last page of his newspaper everything he knew as well as his life and memories. In the last dream where faded roses, fallen leaves, and the dry well in the extensive garden are described, I know you will find your own story, brother mine! I know you take blood-thinning medication to keep your memory from drying up, and that you spend hours every day lying down with your feet up on the wall in order to force the blood into your brain, pulling your recollections one by one out of that dry dismal well. 'March 16, 1957,' you say to yourself, your head blood-red from hanging down the side of sofa or a bed.... 'On March 16, 1957,' you force yourself to remember, 'I was having lunch with colleagues at the City Grill, when I spoke about the masks that jealousy compels us to wear!' Then, 'Yes, yes,' you say, pushing yourself, 'in May of 1962, after an incredible bout of love at noon, waking up in a house on a back street in Kurtuluş, I told the naked woman lying beside me that the large beauty spots on her skin looked like my stepmother's.' Then you're gripped by a doubt that you will later call 'merciless': Had you said it to her? Or was it to that ivory-skinned woman in the stone house where the interminable noise of Beşiktaş Market came in through the windows that didn't close snugly? Or to the misty-eyed woman who, daring to return home late to her husband and children, left the one-room house overlooking Cihangir Park where the trees were naked and trekked all the way to Beyoğlu, just because she loved you so much, to get you the lighter which, as you would later write, you didn't know why you demanded so capriciously? Give me your address and I'll bring you the latest European drug called Mnemonics which opens slam-blam brain vessels clogged with nicotine and horrible memories, taking us instantly back to our lives in the paradise we have lost. After you start taking twenty drops of the lavender liquid in your tea in the morning, not ten as instructed in the package insert, you will remember a lot of the memories you'd forgotten forever, and which you had even forgotten that you'd forgotten, like the colored pencils, combs, and lavender-colored marbles of childhood which suddenly turn up behind an old cupboard. If you let me have your address, you will remember your column—as well as why you wrote it—regarding maps that can be read on all our faces, teeming with signs of compelling locations in the city where we live. If you give me your address, you will remember why you were forced to tell in your column the Rumi's story about the competition between two ambitious painters. If you give me your address, you will remember why you wrote that incomprehensible column saying that there can be no hopeless solitude since even when we are the loneliest, the women of our daydreams keep us company; what's more, that these women who are always intuitively aware of our fantasies wait for us, look for us, and some of them even find us. Give me your address, and let me remind you of what you cannot remember; brother mine, you are now slowly losing the Heaven and Hell that you've lived and dreamed. Give me your address, I'll hurry and save you before your memory sinks into oblivion's bottomless well. I know everything about you, I've read all that you've written: there's no one besides me who can re-create that world so that you can again write those magical texts which glide like predatory eagles over the country by day, and like cunning ghosts at night. When I come to you, you will resume writing pieces which kindle the hearts of young men in coffee-houses in the most forlorn places in Anatolia, which make tears flow like rain down the cheeks of primary-school teachers and their students in the boondocks, which awaken the joy of life in young mothers who live on back streets in small towns reading photo-novels and waiting for death. Give me your address: We'll talk all night and you will regain your tender love for this land and for this people, as well as for your lost past. Think of the down-trodden who write you letters from snow-covered mountain towns where the mail cart stops only once every two weeks; think of the bewildered who write you asking your advice before leaving their fiancées, before going on pilgrimage, before casting their votes in general elections; think of the unhappy students who read you sit-ting in the last row in geography class, the pitiful dispatch clerks glancing at your column sitting at a desk in some obscure corner while they wait for their retirement, the hapless who'd have noth-ing to talk about besides what's on the radio, were it not for your columns. Think of all those reading you at unsheltered bus stops, in the sad, dirty foyers of movie theaters, in remote train stations. They're all waiting for you to perform a miracle, all of them! You have no choice but to provide them with their miracle. Give me your address; two heads are better than one at this. Write telling them the day of redemption is at hand, telling them the days of waiting in line with plastic cans in their hands to get water at the neighborhood fountain will soon be over, telling them it's possi-ble for runaway high-school girls to avoid Galata whorehouses and become movie stars, telling them post-miracle National Lottery tickets will all carry prizes, telling them when husbands come home dead drunk they won't beat their wives, telling them extra car-riages will be put on commuter trains following the day of the mir-acle, telling them that bands will play in all town squares as in those in Europe; write that one day everyone will be a famous hero, and that one day, soon, as well as everyone getting to sleep with any woman he wants including his own mother, everyone will be able to resume considering—magically—the woman with whom he has slept an angelic virgin and a sister. Write and tell them that the code of the secret documents unraveling the historic mystery which has led us into misery for centuries has finally been cracked; tell them that a popular movement networked all over Anatolia is about to take action, and that the homos, priests, bankers, and whores who've organized the international conspiracy condemning us to poverty, and their local collaborators, have been named. Point out their enemies to them, so they can be comforted by knowing who to blame for their desperate lot; let them sense what they can do to rid themselves of their foes, so they can imagine, even as they tremble with rage and sorrow, that one of these days they can accomplish something great; explain to them thoroughly that the cause of their lifelong misery is these repulsive enemies, so they can feel the peace of mind that comes from dumping their sins on others. Brother mine, I know your pen is mighty enough to realize not only all these dreams but even more unbelievable tales and the most unlikely miracles. You will bring the dreams to life with wonderful words and incredible recollections that you'll pull out of the bottomless well of your memory. If our attar from Kars has been able to know the colors of the streets where you spent your childhood, it's only because he could perceive these dreams in between your lines; give him back his dreams. Once upon a time you'd written lines that sent chills down the spines of the unfortunate people in this land, making their hair stand on end, stirring their memories and giving them a taste of the marvelous times to come by reminding them of festival days of yore with their swings and merry-go-rounds. Give me your address and you can do it again. In this wretched country, what can someone like you do besides write? I know you write out of helplessness because you are unable to do anything else. Ah, how often I've contemplated your helpless moments! You felt excruciated seeing pictures of pashas and fruit hanging in green groceries; you felt saddened seeing fierce-eyed but pitiful brothers playing cards in coffeehouses with decks pasty from sweat. Whenever I saw a mother and son get in line in front of the State Meat and Fish Foundation at the crack of dawn, hoping to do their shopping on the cheap, or whenever my train went by small clearings in the morning where workers' markets had been set up, or whenever my eye caught fathers who sat on Sunday afternoons with their wives and children in treeless parks without a blade of green, smoking and waiting for the end of the eternal hour of boredom, I often wondered what you *thought* about these people. Had you seen all the scenes I observed? I knew you would've written their stories on white paper that absorbed the ink when you returned home to your tiny room in the evening to sit at your time-worn desk which was totally appropriate to this pitiful, forgotten land. I'd imagine your head bending over the paper and conjure up the image of you rising from your desk around midnight, feeling sick at heart, to open the refrigerator, as you had once written, and look in absentmindedly without touching or seeing anything, and then how you walked around the rooms and the desk like a somnambulist. Ah, my brother, you were alone, you were pitiful, you were sad. How I loved you! I thought of you, only you, when I read all you'd written all these years. Please, give me your address; at least give me an answer. I'll tell you how I saw letters that were stuck like dead spiders on the faces of some cadets from the War College whom I'd come across on the Yalova boat, and when I got those robust cadets alone in the filthy head on board how they were beset by a sweet childlike dread. I'll tell you how the blind lottery-man who, after drinking a shot of *raki*, had his tavern companions read the letters he got from you that he carried in his pocket, proudly pointing out the mystery between the lines which you'd divulged to him, and how he had his son read him the *Milliyet* every morning to find the sentence which would clinch the mystery. His letters carried the stamp of the Teşvikiye Post Office. Hello, are you listening to me? At least, say something; let me know you're there. Oh my God! I hear you breathe, I hear your breathing. Listen: I've taken great pains composing these sentences, so listen carefully: When you wrote that the narrow smoke-stacks on old harbor ferryboats letting out melancholic trails of smoke seemed so delicate and breakable, I understood you. When you wrote that you suddenly couldn't breathe at provincial weddings where the women danced with the women and the men with the men, I understood you. About that movie featuring Hercules, Samson, or Roman history which you saw at the sort of theater where small children sell secondhand *Texas* and *Tom Mix* comics at the door, when you wrote that you were so confounded by the silence that fell over the theater pulsating with men as soon as a third-class American movie star with a dolorous face and long legs put in an appearance on the screen that you wanted to die, I understood you. How about that? Do you understand me? Answer me, you wretch! I am that incredible reader any writer would consider himself lucky to run across even if only once in his lifetime! Give me your address and I'll bring you photos of high-school girls who adore you, all hundred and twenty-seven of them, some with their addresses on the back and others with their adulation as quoted in their journals. Thirty-two of them wear glasses, eleven have braces on their teeth, six have long swanlike necks, twenty-four of them sport ponytails just as you fancy. They're all crazy about you, they think you're to die for. I swear it. Give me your address and I'll bring you a list of women each of whom was wholeheartedly convinced that you meant her in a conversational column you wrote in the early sixties, saying, 'Listen to the radio last night? Well, listening to "Lovers' Hour," I myself could only think of one thing.' You have as many admirers in high-society circles as you do among army wives and infatuated highstrung students in their provincial or white-collar homes. Did you know that? If you let me have your address, I'd bring you photos of women in disguise, masquerading not only for those sad society balls but in their daily private lives. You'd once written, rightly so, that we have no private lives, that we don't even have any real comprehension of the concept of 'private life' which we appropriated from translated novels and foreign publications, but if you could just see these photos taken in high-heeled boots and devil's masks, well... Oh, come on, give me that address, I beg you. I'll bring you my incredible collection of human faces I've been saving up for the last twenty years. I have pictures of jealous lovers taken immediately after they've destroyed each others' faces with nitric acid. I have bewildered-looking mug shots of bearded or clean-shaven fundamentalists caught conducting secret rites for which they'd painted Arabic letters on their faces, of Kurdish rebels where the letters on their faces had been burned away by napalm, execution photos of rapists who are hanged hush-hush in provincial towns which I got by bribing my way into their official files. Contrary to the depictions in cartoons, when the greased noose snaps the neck, the tongue doesn't stick out. But the letters become more legible. Now I know what secret compulsion drove you to write in an old column that you preferred old-style executions and executioners. Just as I know you go in for ciphers, acrostics, cryptograms, I also know you walk among us in the middle of the night wearing just the sort of costume to reestablish the lost mystery. I'm onto what shenanigans you pull on the lawyer husband to get your half sister alone and trash everything all night for the sake of telling the simplest story that makes us who we are. When, in response to the lawyers' wives who wrote angry letters about your bits ridiculing lawyers, you said that the lawyer in question didn't happen to be their husband, I knew you were telling the truth. It's high time you gave me your address. I know all the individual significances of those dogs, skulls, horses, and witches whooping it up in your dreams, and I also know which love missives you were inspired into writing by the tiny pictures of women, guns, skulls, soccer players, flags, flowers that cab drivers stick in the corner of their rearview mirrors. I know quite a lot of the code sentences you dole out to your pitiful admirers just to get rid of them; and I also know you never part with the notebook in which those key sentences are written, nor with your historical costumes. . . . "

Much later, long after Galip had pulled the phone cord out of the jack and searched through his notebooks, old costumes, closets and worked like a somnambulist looking for his memories, lying in his bed wearing his pajamas and listening to night noises in Nişantaşi, he understood once more, as he fell into a long and deep sleep, that the capital aspect of sleep was—aside from forgetting the heartbreaking distance between who a person was and who he believed he could someday become—peacefully scrambling together all that he'd heard and all that he hadn't, all that he'd seen and all that he hadn't, all that he knew and all that he did not.

Marcel Duchamp:
The Woolworth Building
as Readymade,
January 1916

(An Approximation)

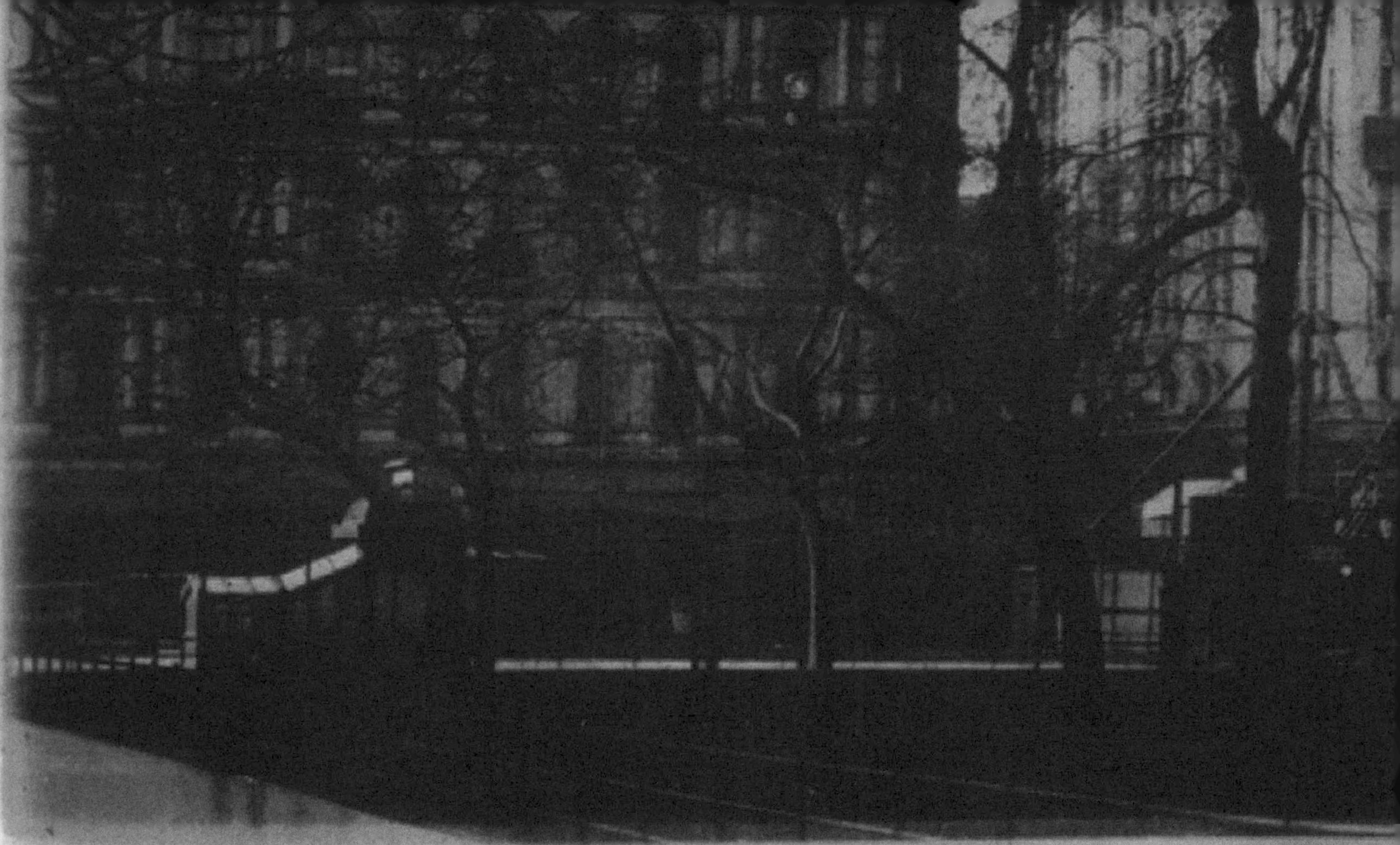

P1562 Woolworth Building, (75 ©

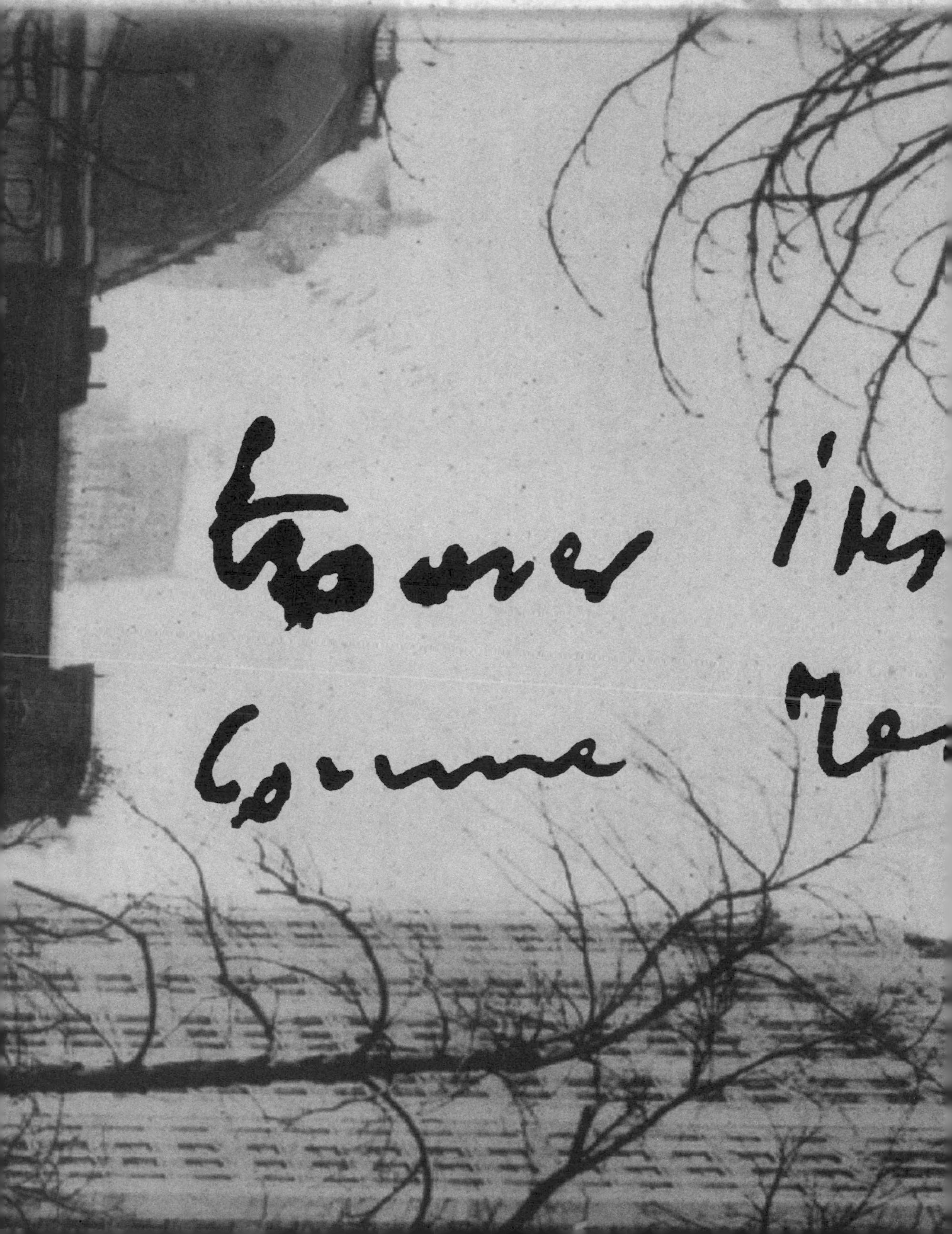

...cription for ...

...ady made —

Apropos: of Readymades

In 1913 Marcel Duchamp mounted a bicycle wheel on a wooden stool in his Paris studio. The resulting work, *The Bicycle Wheel*, inaugurated a series of seemingly ordinary objects, appropriated from the everyday, which consciously challenged the divide between fine art and mass production, between high culture and low. More than any other work of twentieth-century art, perhaps, these objects epitomized the cultural transition from the Industrial Revolution to the Postmodern era.

But it was not until later, in 1915, during his sojourn in New York, that Duchamp would give this series the designation by which it is now known: readymades. The year after his arrival, in a letter to his sister Suzanne dated January 1916, he alluded to the full implication of both *The Bicycle Wheel* and his second readymade, *The Bottle Rack*, referring to them for the first time as "readymades" and asking that she be sure to save them. Living in New York may have had a galvanizing effect on Duchamp and his work. The bulk of his readymade series was conceived and produced there from 1915 on.

In the same month that he sent his letter to Suzanne, Duchamp wrote the following note on a sheet of paper: *Trouver inscription pour Woolworth Bldg comme readymade*— ("Find inscription for Woolworth Bldg as readymade—"). At 750 feet, Cass Gilbert's Woolworth Building was, at the time, the world's tallest building. In a purely conceptual act, Duchamp seems to have appropriated the Woolworth Building as the largest readymade. In keeping with Duchamp's strategy of using time as a constructive element in art, however, this imperative was not published until fifty years later when it appeared in *The White Box*, the third and last publication of Duchamp's notes during his lifetime. This portfolio attempts to put Duchamp's idea back into the circuits of discourse.

To Draw The Blinds

To draw the blinds down,
                                            as
late as possible,   almost
too late
              so I won't miss
the last dark blue light,
                                    last outline
of the muffled bushes,
                          trees absorbed
                          by
the sky's last lingering,
                            uncurling still
its fingers from our handclasp,
                            the leaves' patterns pressing
                            toward me
It is to make the day last,   to stand on
an edge,   a brink of
separation,   daring
to be seen by whatever stranger may
look in from the outside, even
the street, the road,   to partake of
the stranger's eyes — while
the lamps are unlit still — the stranger
looking in   with
the onrush of the hours.
                                    I'm
straddling two kingdoms,   one leg on
either bankside.

I'm daring
these minutes to take leave of me.
                              They hold me
to the window   They lean into it
as I lean out as far as possible,
the curving line of treetops
sloping to the window,

                    the dark between us
                    looking both ways,

at me, & away,   I
swing on it,   I am both ways,
my timing doubles,

              the blade dropping
till it cuts me down.

Panther

In the 1970s, unlike most of my platformed peers with whom I spent many semiconscious hours smoking cannabis by the bale, I was not given to dreamlike reveries of floating across the Peruvian pinkflaked cliffs of Superfly Valhalla with a mink-lined cape billowing off my shoulder. Nor did I boast aspirations of cruising in the rabbit-fur comfort of a customized El-D with a stable of hypnotized ho's under my charismatic control.

No, my idea of a good time was parading through the streets with Nixon's maimed, dog-jowled head speared on the end of a bayonet. I wanted to live on the streets described in the pages of *The East Village Other**, join a cell of the Weather Underground, then blow up buildings, assassinate heads of state, and pollute the

---

* *The East Village Other* was the one consoling publication of my teenhood. It was a mad mix of comix, poetry, and politics celebrating all those values close to the hearts of disenchanted American youth: antiauthoritarianism, unrestricted drug use, unrestrained (and latex-free) fornication and savage rock 'n' roll. *EVO*'s founding contributors included Ishmael Reed, David Henderson (under the pseudonym "D.B. (Dark Brown) Rice"), and Steve Cannon, author of the Olympia Press classic *Groove, Bang and Jive Around*. As *EVO* was a publication identified with the Lower East Side's drop-out whyte community, the contributions of these and other black writers to its pages are significant, especially given the black literary presence in New York and the Lower East Side in particular, and the continuing impact of these writers on American "alternative" culture.

water supply with the finest LSD the chemical underground had to offer.

But until the revolution came, I was forced to wait in the basement of my father's house on a secondhand Castro Convertible sofa under posters of Angela Davis and H. Rap Brown, a square of paper acid dissolving on my tongue, and watch Universal's old monster movies on a flea-market Motorola. Or I could be found in the company of my comrades, Huck 'n' Pete, with the Last Poets and the Funkadelics rasping through cheap speakers in the background, smoking one clumsily rolled joint after the other, reading Uncle Ho Chi Minh on guerrilla warfare, plotting our high school's takeover and destruction.

Pete 'n' I stayed up until four in the morning, after an exhausting day of getting high in high school, and a longer night of getting blasted in the basement, sitting in the front room of his parents' house, talking and listening to jazz, concocting meals out of whatever we found moldering in the rear of his mother's refrigerator, drowning it in hot sauce before it had a chance to crawl out of our plates.

The alarm buzzed at 6:45 each morning. I awoke to a Fleischer Bros. cartoon on the tube and a stick of the one-poke pot I pilfered from my father's upstairs stash. As Koko the Clown jumped out of the inkwell singing those *St. James Infirmary Blues*, I dressed in ragged bellbottoms, needle-toed cowboy boots, and a red-fisted Columbia STRIKE! T-shirt, with a crash helmet hanging off my belt loop.

By 7:15, Huck and I had hooked up to get fucked up. Huck was six foot one of solid bushy-headed Negro with the kind of attitude that would put most black men behind bars. But not him. On the lapel of his pea coat, he wore a button lifted from the cover art of Miles Davis's *On the Corner* album. It read "Free Me." He said it meant he was a political prisoner without a prison. As soon as Huck and I had locked the joint's stub in the vise of two paper matchsticks and scorched it with flame, there was Pete, the neighborhood's b-ball coolie, listing forward with his mouth open and his lips stretched out, ready to suck in and share the fumes.

Afterward the three of us joined the remainder of our crew on the corner, slouching against the slats of a white picket fence. There was hook-nosed "Watts," a self-described "black militant" and scowling Lilliputian with a monster-sized 'fro, nicknamed after he raised a riot in our school cafeteria: Bouncing up and down in white Converse sneakers, he had sliced the air with the teeth of a metal Afro-pick and hurled a volley of greasy meatballs, shouting "DEATH TO ALL Y'ALL DEGENERATE, NO-TASTIN', POTATO-SALAD-EATIN' HONKY DEVILS!" There was the impeccably dressed, and self-assuredly *cool* "Honey Boy Tuna," a Seventh-Day Adventist who wanted to be a pimp; and the three-hundred-pound "Pork Rind," who looked like a gelatinous mold of head cheese in blue overalls, black leather coat, and wide-brim straw fedora with a pair of tinted granny glasses perched on his nose, munching from an ever-present bag of Howard's barbecue-flavored pig skins.

To my chagrin my friends had not apposed an appropriate appellation to my person, a name suiting my revolutionary persona (say, "Chairman Ho Chi Nigget") No. Instead, they called me "Wolfman"—that hairy howling lunatic who crept on raised canine arches. Their reasons were two-fold:

1. I had a reputation for talking mucho shit ("wolfin'" (as in "The Boy Who Cried Wolf") the would be Don Corleone whyte boys with the greased-back hair who crowded around the water fountain outside the cafeteria.

2. As a child, I wanted to join the ranks of screen legends Boris Karloff, Peter Lorre, and Vincent Price. I wanted to be "The World's First Horror-Movie Kiddie Star" and appear in films with titles like *Blood-Shriek of the Buck-Dancing Pickaninny* (a sure-fire favorite with the hillbilly halfwits on the southern drive-in circuit).

So, spotting an ad in the rear of *Monster Times* which promised to reveal the secrets of lycanthropic transformation, I mailed five dollars to a P.O. Box in Derby, CT and received, for my troubles, a set of plastic, glow-in-the-dark dog dentures.

Undeterred by this blatant act of mail fraud, I utilized instead the skills gleaned from a special Dick Smith edition of the *Monster Make-up Handbook* (with step-by-step instructions on how to turn yourself into one of Big Daddy Roth's pop-eyed, razor-toothed demons with some nose putty, a little mortician's wax, and two halves of a ping-pong ball). With a mournful howl, I'd leap from a limb of the maple tree in front of my house and pounce on one of my unsuspecting playmates, my face clotted with clumps of hair saved from my last haircut and a mucusy mixture of spirit gum and water.

It was a period in my life no one ever let me forget. By the time I was nine years old, I'd become a local legend. Even now, over thirty years later, strange children approach me on my occasional visits home, their eyes wide with curiosity and fear, asking, "Is it true you be the Wolfman of Winchester Avenue?"

In the early '70s, the Black Panther Party's ideology, analysis, and rhetoric gave definition to, and provided a vocabulary for, the anger, frustration, and confusion I and others of my generation felt in the aftermath of the 1950s and '60s civil rights battles.

Through elementary and junior high school, we had experienced the full trauma of the '60s. America's public institutions did not, and could not, provide us with the tools to understand the glaring absurdity of being black in the exclusionary environment of mainstream culture. Our so-called "race leaders" did not speak to us. Instead, their language was tempered for the sensibilities of monied white liberalism. We were forced to seek self-illumination elsewhere.

The tube signaled our first moment of deepening self worth: It was the loud proud black man who exclaimed: *I am the Greatest!* He shocked America. Black and white alike.

Who this nigger say he pretty? *Little Richard?*

Lawd! Who dis nigga talk like dat in front all dem whyte folks? He gwine git us *lainched* fo' sho'!

Our second was Kwame Touré's clarion call of BLACK POWER! in Greenwood, Mississippi; followed by H. Rap Brown, in his way-cool Wayfarers, singing back-up doo-wops on *Burn, Baby, Burn*; and the third was the whyte-ass-kicking antics of Kato on *The Green Hornet*.

Otherwise, we cast a cynical eye on the culture.

Once, a classroom discussion of a current-events cartoon in *My Weekly Reader* nearly came to all-out blows ("Buffy the Bear be talkin' shit! What he mean 'get off the welfare'? We gon' bust Buffy in his fuzzy, honey-eatin' behind!"), so our teacher decided a formal debate was best.

When called upon to choose sides, I raised my hand and, as the Molotov-cocktail-tossing cadres of doo-ragged doo-woppers in those really cool shades seemed a far more attractive choice than the nonviolent, spiritual-singing marchers I watched get head-whipped, fire-hosed, and laughed at on television (an awful lot of trouble to go through for the right to sit next to the whyte man in a deseg-regated toilet stall), I joined the all-black, preteen pro-"militant" squad, proposing we pool our resources with our red-skinned sis-tern and brethren and take back the *whole* red, white, and blue muthafucka!!!

I first suspected something was up in the fourth grade. Amerikkka began to smell funky after Dallas, but I under-stood the bullet in Kennedy's head.

The man was a sitting duck: his teeth clenched in a big Pep-sodent smile, his arms waving like a mechanical dummy encased in a glass booth at a seaside arcade, exposed to thousands in the back of a stretch limo with the roof down. Then *bull's-eye*!!! Brain bits all over Jackie's pillbox.

But Oswald? *Shot? On national television?* Surrounded by hun-dreds of *cops*! I WASN'T BUYIN' IT!!! To my nine-year-old brain, it seemed Kennedy had been dead but five minutes before some red-nosed peckawood hauled Oswald out in front of the news cameras, talking 'bout, "This man killed the president!

I was watching television, pissed off I was missing my afternoon Popeye cartoons, snacking on a chocolate duck-doodle, staring at this squinty-eyed peckawood in a fucked-up cowboy hat, and the only thoughts I had were, "How you know?" and "How you find him so fast?"

I might have been a cartoon-watchin', grape-Kool-Aid-drinkin', monster-model-makin', little colored boy chumped into thinking he was actually a werewolf by a five-dollar set of plastic dog-den-tures, BUT I WASN'T A GODDAMNED FOOL!!!

Oswald said, "I didn't do it. I've been set up. I'm a patsy." I be-lieved him. Then he was shot. In the "protective custody" of the police. Watching his murder, I experienced the same horror, the same fear I felt the first time I saw photos of Emmett Till's corpse in *Ebony* magazine.

Unconsciously, I transshaped the two images in the suffocat-ing detail of dreamscape: the charred, mutilated genitalia of Till's corpse with Oswald's winded death-fall. For a black, male child experiencing the world before the Civil Rights Act and the Voting Rights Bill were even signed into legislation, whistling at whyte girls was tantamount to killing the president—castration anxiety, indeed!

After the country's "official" period of mourning, the nation resumed its business and the authorities in my elementary school made an attempt at dealing with the emotional trauma this public tragedy might have on our young psyches by inviting a psychologist from the city's Department of Public Health to conduct classroom discussions on the president's assassination.

The health department's visiting psychologist was escorted into the classroom by Miss Fishbox, the school principal, an elderly whyte woman with the Cold War's A-bomb-shelter mentality. The psychologist looked like a dim-witted gym instructor. He had the conical, barrel-chested build of a turnip on steroids, his look of dimness emphasized by a swollen Joe Palooka jaw. And he wore his hair in that by-product of Peace Corps liberalism, the "folk-a-nanny" crewcut, hair that said, Burl Ives is hip!

He smiled and tried to initiate discussion. Understandably, my classmates, confused and numb with shock, sat in silence. Though saddened by the president's passing, I raised my hand and voiced my fears regarding the suspicious circumstances of Oswald's murder. The psychologist grinned in open-mouthed disbelief. His tongue protruded to the right and his eyes cut to the left. Miss Fishbox's liver-spotted face pinched in hostility. She told me to shut up.

I was just the attention-seeking class crackpot, a crackpot spawned of "bohemian" parents, who wasted his time tinkering with nightmare face makeup in his father's sculpting studio, brought in photos of his experiments for show-and-tell, and made his classmates puke their undigested cornflakes and chocolate peanut butter cups on their wooden desktops.

Miss Fishbox's face turned a mottled high-blood-pressure purple. She wagged her finger. I was that "colored" child who watched violent monster movies in a musty basement and thought he was a werewolf. What possible trauma could he suffer watching that pathetic communist Lee Harvey Oswald get what he deserved on national television?

Her face returned to its normal shade of jellyfish gray. The psychologist's brow lumped in furrowed concentration. Then, brightly, he reminded me that this was still America and not Russia. In Russia, he said, po' liddle cullud kidz like me can't grow up with the same equal opportunity to become the first Colored Werewolf

President of the United States like we do in America no matter how much of the whyte folks' welfare money we cullud folks done spent.

"Let me ask you zomethin'," he said. "Do you like vodka?"

"Huh? Uh—*no*! My Daddy drinks rum!"

"Well," he continued, "you're gonna learn to like it if the commies ever take over. 'Cause that's all you're gonna get. No more fried chicken and 'gator ribs with corn-liquor gravy or whatever it is you people eat! Just vodka! Breakfast, lunch, and dinner!

"In a communist-controlled America," he said, "baseball cards would be replaced by *Heroes of the People's Revolution* trading cards, you'll be passing around pictures of that butcher Joe Stalin instead of Willie Mays! Popeye would be carted out in tar and feathers, denounced as a lackey dupe of the military-industrial complex, and his cartoons would be preempted by the wacky misadventures of Mao Tse-tung."

My classmates shivered with the fear of God.

"Not only that, you'll own only one pair of cloth shoes, manufactured in Communist China, and work eighteen hours a day, including Sunday, because goin' to church will be against the law in Communist America, punishable by death! And do you know what you'll be doing during those hard eighteen hours a day? Wanna take a guess?"

I shrugged my shoulders. "Nope."

"Making vodka! And that's what that weasly little commie Oswald was trying to do! Take over America and force poor little colored children like you to be alcoholic slaves to the State!"

By 1970—stoned, cynical, and Apple Jack–capped—we had wiped our asses with the pages of America's history books. We had seen this country for what it was: a lie. It was thanks to the legacy of Malcolm X*, which formed the basis of the Black Panther Party, that we could perceive, analyze, and articulate the ways we had been hurt by the lies perpetuated in those institutions.

Through Malcolm, the Black Panther Party had given us a language to clarify our circumstances, an arsenal of ideas to guide us

---

* I'm often asked what I thought of Spike's *X*, and I reply that I'm waiting for the sequel, *XII*, starring Bo Derek with an extra pair of tits.

Darius James, 1970.

toward an understanding of who we were, a "revolutionary" sense of self in the face of an oppressive culture. For many, including myself, it was the first time in our lives we spoke with authenticity.

Pick up the gun! and *Off the pig!* was the language we spoke. For 1970s black youth, the Panthers served the same critical function as rap music does for today's hip-hop young. The Black Panthers were our Public Enemy, both figuratively and literally, declared so by that shame of the American transvestite community, FBI head J. Edgar Hoover.

The Panthers weren't academics, coffeehouse intellectuals, or opportunists with six-figure record deals. The Panthers were a product of the streets. The Panthers spoke the language of the streets and their words were reinforced by deeds. And, in their deeds, they were intent on responding to the needs of the people in the streets.

Huey Newton and Bobby Seale began the Party as a reaction to their disgust for the theorizing, inactivity, and coffeehouse rambling of the Merritt College African American Association's armchair revolutionaries. Together, they spoke to Oakland's black community in order to determine their exact needs and desires, and on October 15th, 1966, they finalized the Black Panther Party's "declaration of black empowerment," the *Ten Point Program and Platform: What We Want, What We Believe.*

As Elaine Brown restated, in brief, in *A Taste of Power*, the Black Panthers demanded "restitution for slavery, food, education, decent housing and land for black people . . .; [that] constitutional guarantees relating to 'justice for all' be enforced for blacks; the exemption of blacks from the military service; the release of all black prisoners and the granting of new trials by juries of their peers." And lastly, it "stated that blacks in America had the right to self-determination and called for a U.N.–supervised plebiscite to establish this claim." It was published on the back page of each issue of the Party's newspaper.

On the Bay Area college circuit, Huey and Bobby met with resistance in their drive to recruit membership for the Party. They found their greatest support on the street. "Lil' Bobby" Hutton was their first recruit.

Seventeen months later, two days after Martin Luther King was assassinated on the balcony of a hot-sheet motel in Memphis, Lil' Bobby was gunned down in a battle with the Oakland police. He was only seventeen.

I was thirteen the first time I came in contact with the Panthers. I had written a play called *Panther*. It was an abstract history of black oppression in America, culminating in the formation of the Black Panther Party.

I'd been encouraged to write the play by Walter Dallas, a graduate student in Yale's School of Drama. He in turn introduced me to Black Panther Erica Huggins, widow of Black Panther John Huggins, captain of the Southern California chapter of the Party. John Huggins was murdered by a member of the United Slaves posse at U.C.L.A. He was killed two days after a dispute between the black students of U.C.L.A. and the United Slaves over who would determine the direction of the new Black Studies program in 1969—a program that the United Slaves' despot and architect of the faux-African holiday, Kwanza Ron Karenga, attempted to usurp.

I remember Ms. Huggins as a tall, regal, and charming woman. She smiled. I flirted. We talked about my play. She said it was a counter-revolutionary product of cultural nationalism.

"—but I can *correct* that, young *bleed*!"

She escorted me to the basement of the local branch of the Black Panther Party, gave me a stack of the Party's newspapers and told me to read them. I did.

One week later she was in jail, charged with murder.

After that first encounter, and throughout my first years in high school, I sold the Party's newspapers, collected contributions for the Panthers' free breakfast program and legal defense fund, organized "political education" workshops, and was busted for burning a nineteen-cent American flag. Eventually the F.B.I.'s Fred MacMurray lookalikes bugged my phone under its COINTELPRO program.*

In the summer of 1970, before entering our freshman year of high school, Huck, Pete, and I camped on the lawn of the New Haven Green, across the street from the Superior Court-house, attending daily prisoner-support rallies for Black Panther Lonnie McLucas, who was to go on trial with eleven other members of the Party—including Erica Huggins and cofounder, chairman, and cookbook author "Barbecuin' with Bobby" Seale—for the kidnap, torture, and murder of suspected police-informant Alex Rackley.

We lounged in a stuporous fog of cheap wine and pot smoke: I strained my eyes staring at the nipples of braless hippie women; Pete pondered the life of Ho Chi Minh; and Huck complained about "the songs." It was the same song he said, playing over and over again.

"Which one?"

"*Sugar Sugar*, by the fuckin' Archies!"

Huck intercepted phantom radio signals, a peculiar side effect he experienced after smoking pot. It never happened to him after he dropped acid or nodded out on reds. His teeth were in great shape so he couldn't attribute it to metal fillings. How else could he explain the voice of the Arizona John Bircher he once heard

---

* And logged hundreds of hours of my failed attempts to bed the enchanting Melissa Marlowe! What I did with my circumcised teenage penis cost the American taxpayer thousands of dollars in equipment and man-hours and was a matter of grave security to Nixon's United States. Sadly, however, Melissa was not meant to be. She brought me home and introduced me to her alcoholic mom and stiff-necked dad, two figures from a Norman Rockwell still-life. "He's a genius," Melissa said. "BUT HE'S BLACK!" they said. "And that's the end of that," I said.

buzzing in his skull through a wall of white noise, accusing a prominent black civil rights leader of being a puppet of the International Zionist conspiracy?

I'd just returned to New Haven after spending two semesters at a boys boarding school in the woodlands of western Massachusetts. As I was not the kind of Negro who knew how to dribble a basketball, nor did my family have any money (I was a pearl-diving kitchen slave on financial aid), and given, too, that I flashed during my preacceptance interview, much to my mother's dismay, a vinyl-covered copy of Mao Tse-tung's *Little Red Book* of quaint communist quotations, I have no idea why I was let loose among these people. But there I was, in the thick of starched-white and blue-blazered New England Preppiedom, higher than a Chinese box-kite, spouting the incendiary rhetoric of armed insurrection with my teenage testicles dangling from the holes worn through the crotch of my denim bellbottoms.

I spent that summer, along with Huck 'n' Pete, under the Viet Cong colored banner of the "New Haven Wino Liberation Front," in the circle of wine-and-reefer-anointed acolytes of "Professor" Herman Wilson. Professor Wilson, tall, brown, and bald with a scrub of nappy salt-and-pepper growth on his chin, conducted, while copping spare coin for "the revolutionary's weapon of choice" (a cold pint of Thunderbird wine), open-air lectures or, to the uninitiated, free-form harangues, on the insidious ensnarements awaiting the black man in Amerikkkan society:

"Light bulbs, got any ideas where the expression 'the wellsprings of wisdom' comes from?"

"Um . . . a fountain of knowledge?"

"Just another cliché for the same." He searched our faces and found nothing.

"Give up? Okay, let's look at the word *academe*—" Then he turned around to address a businessman, pointing his finger, with spittle gathered under his lower lip.

"Hey, you in the glasses! Yeah, I'm talkin' to you!"

The businessman stopped, frightened.

"I would like to raise your reduced consciousness to this hard revolutionary fact o' life: It's your *duty* and *obligation* to both our sacred mother planet and the future of the human race to contribute whatever monies you have to a special slush fund for this coterie of fine young revolutionaries. *Or we'll kill you.*"

Herman continued, counting quarters. "For the ancient Greeks, the place of learning was a grove near Athens called an 'academe' (or, as I prefer to think, where Plato drank wine, got wasted, and talked shit). This 'academe' of trees and flowers surrounded a body of water.

"So, the distinctive feature of an academy is that it surrounds a body of water, supporting and nourishing *life*. Thus, the expression 'the wellsprings of wisdom!'" He pointed to Yale's Old Campus across the Green.

"Now look at that stone fortress across the street. Do you have any idea what lies in its center? What makes up its heart?" We stared, our expressions blank, our eyes red.

"A Goddamned *cemetery*!" he spat. "Yale University is built around a *bone yard*!"

"Git da wine, Herman! And stop talkin' crazy!"

"Fuck the wine! This is a lesson in the revolutionary's first code of conduct—*Know Your Enemy*!"

"But we don't be understannin' what you be sayin' Herman! Break da shit down fo' us."

"Do I have to spoon-feed you simpletons? What I'm saying is this: those freakish Dr. Strangelove muthafuckas coming out of Yale are going to control the world's major corporations, commit mass genocide, and fuck the corpses! Why do you think there's so much secrecy shrouding that death's-head-in-tuxedo Skull 'n' Bones cabal? Do you think it's only a mover-up for frat boys having fun with the sororities' underwear? Use what brains you have left! It's bigger than that—*it's a conspiracy!* From Nixon on down."

"I hear you, Herman!" I piped. "'Cause if you remember *Dracula*—"

"C'mon, Herman! We don't wanna hear dis shit! Git us some *grape*!"

"Let the brutha speak, picklehead!"

"Well, uh, if we apply a correct Marxist analysis to Stoker's text, who I believe was associated with both the Fabians, and the Golden Dawn, and understand its occult as well as its Marxist shadings, you'll see that the aristocracy, or the military industrial complex's capitalist ruling class of Dracula's time, is a class of walking dead, feeding—*vampirically*—on the life energy, or blood, of the peasant-lumpen classes."

"Dis nigga crazier than you, Herman!"

"Shut up! Let him speak!"

"Now we need only extrapolate on Stoker's basic theory of the vampiric nature of the ruling class, and look at the class-structure of the Undead (the vampire being the capitalist taskmaster, the zombie being the exploited worker, and the ghoul representing the lumpen underclass), then concretely apply his theory to our current condition of oppression, vis-à-vis Yale's bone yard, and take proper revolutionary measures."

"Right on young bruthd I'm sure you'll git plenty wimmins wid dat rap! Now git da wine sofu' body, *please!*"

Little Golden Aquariums

*. . . of those that are drawn away, each
is drawn elsewhere toward another.*

James Agee

the families living
through each depression
too young to know
directly but through
grandparents mother
and Tom some how
the days were time
pleasure in company
of each

having the party
always behind house
away from the road

dark to bed girls
with their sisters
brothers so John Daddy
with Floy til sun

children leave as
time WW II pulled
to work or nation
some never returning
to the farm

took their picture
children together on
railroad tracks
showing their future
how to get there

My Education
A Book of Dreams

Airport. Like a high school play, attempting to convey a spectral atmosphere. One desk onstage, a gray woman behind the desk with the cold waxen face of an intergalactic bureaucrat. She is dressed in a gray-blue uniform. Airport sounds from a distance, blurred, incomprehensible, then suddenly loud and clear. "Flight sixty-nine has been—" Static... fades into the distance... "Flight..."

Standing to one side of the desk are three men, grinning with joy at their prospective destinations. When I present myself at the desk, the woman says: "You haven't had your education yet."

This dream occurred approximately thirty-five years ago, shortly after the publication of *Naked Lunch* with the Olympia Press in Paris in 1959.

For years I wondered why dreams are so often so dull when related, and this morning I find the answer, which is very simple—like most answers, you have always known it: *No context*... like a stuffed animal set on the floor of a bank.

Survival is the name of the game, William. The scruffiest hippie is my messenger... do not expect radiant messengers of light. Expect the flawed, the maimed in body and spirit. It's all a film run backward... the Atom Bomb through Manhattan to the formula... $E = MC^2$.

New York City dawn streets. Making my way from downtown back to my hotel in the fifties. Yes, I can feel the key in my pocket. A market where a number of people are emptying garbage bags. A truck is unloading the bags. Someone has found a gun. What a fool to turn it in, I think. Up on the top floor of a high building I can see down a narrow air shaft, pipes and iron ladders five hundred feet down. Why walk? I jump off an iron balcony and swim through the air uptown.

Meet two naked angels about sixteen. They say it's their first solo flight. The city spread out underneath us about a thousand feet down in beautiful pastel shades...all quite idyllic....

One of the boys says he has "lost it" and it is a long way down. [...] I take off into what I now call "*my* element," out through the clouds, and in fact sit down on a cloud, which I can do because I got no weight at all. Just floating, lonely as a cloud, and the view is so breathtaking and no fear of falling anymore. I got no body to fall. Just me and my shadow. Strolling down the avenue over New York.

There is no hurry...no hurry at all.

A big party in NYC. Ian is there and Anne Waldman, the Naropa Mother. You need a place to stay? You got a dose of clap? Take all your troubles to the Naropa Mother. She gives all the satisfaction. I find that I am junk-sick and someone can give me a shot of Jade. We retire to a sort of bathroom with a double partition. I am looking around for a tap and basin, maybe I will have to use water from the toilet, but he brings out ampules in a paper box with directions in green letters. So he takes out a big ampule full of green liquid, loads it into a syringe, and shoots it into my main line at the elbow and my arm swells up and turns purple like when I took the Bogomolets Anti-Human Serum— supposed to make me live to be 125—and I come near getting put in isolation in Panama, where the customs agent didn't half like the look of my arm. I tell him it is just an allergy.

I do notice a distinct sensation as this Jade drains all the way in. Not like junk, more like an injection of stone. Anyhow, stoned, but it isn't pleasant...Lots of people around and each one looks like the other and they have brought some *horrible* food...like raw entrails. This food is gross and there is a nightmare feeling here. Can't find Ian. Don't know how to get home or where home is.

A place to fish at the end of a cobblestone street. Deep blue water. Someone has thrown in a float and it is already bobbing.

Portland Place. Empty house. Leaves blowing, drifting like shreds of time. [...]

Fresh southerly winds. New York. A remote curtained drawing room. Marble mantelpiece. Decanter of port. A table. Maps and blueprints.

"There are many alternatives."

Subways, train stations, airports, boats ... travel, all the time clutching my hotel keys, the only connection I have. The only home I have. I constantly reassure myself by feeling the key there in my pocket. Not that it means very much, since there is no privacy in the area.

Blue used to be my favorite color. Since I have started to paint, it has shown itself as the most difficult color to work with. Blue is unmagical. It is just *blue*; there are no nuances, no extensions. Rarely do figures and faces appear in a blue painting. Just blue on paper and that is all. Very occasionally I get lucky with blue. The association of blue with money. Blue-chip stocks. Cool remote blue boardrooms. And with junk. Cool blue mineral calm. Perhaps blue is a *quantitative* color.

A blue picture I have just completed. I look for some meaning, some life. There is none. The blue paint even clogs the drain in the sink.

Walking in a strange city. I was composing a short story called "The End of the Line." This seemed to be in eastern Siberia, just across the Bering Strait. I arrive with one suitcase and a bottle of morphine pills ... dying of cancer.

Ian and I are in a hospital. He wouldn't, as usual. A large oil painting, brown balloon-shaped figurations crossed with grid in black. Like old hot-air balloons. There are many entries to the Western Lands. The mark is a feeling of serene joy. It may be flash of sunlight on muddy water. A house. A particular house ... the porch made of large yellow stones in a matrix. Iced tea ... calm peace ... another house in North St. Louis ... on a hillside ... a garage ... bits of vivid and vanishing detail. An apartment house ... outskirts of Chicago. Nice Japanese. A sea whiff on the wind was its music. A moving camera. A run-down patio. Bougainvillea. Purple flowers underfoot ... Tangier ... Marrakech ...

Palm Beach, L.A. Tornado watch. Go out rather than take refuge in the flooded basement. Are the pumps holding their own? Remember sea story. Turn on the pumps. We're shipping water and our muscles bulge to tremendous size. Wish I could get down there and pump it out.

There are no innocent bystanders. What were they doing there in the first place? Like the woman who was hit and killed by a fragment from the helicopter that fell over on its side on top of the Pan Am Building. Friends are urging me to use this helicopter, but I have a bad feeling about it. Hell of a location. Suppose it crashes right onto the evening rush at Grand Central? And I quote: "Be not the first by whom the new is tried, nor yet the last to lay the old aside." And sure as shit and taxes this accident happens a week later. The copter has landed and then falls onto its side and kills a nineteen-year-old youth on his way back some-where. And a woman walking along Madison Avenue was hit and killed by a piece of the propeller.

Rilke said: "Give every man his own death." This seems as far as possible from any tailor-made death. She is walking down or up Madison Avenue, after eating in a cafeteria, before eating or shopping. Works there, doesn't work there, way out of orbit there, and suddenly two pounds of metal hit her in the back of the head. What were her last thoughts? The last words in her mind? No one will ever know. [. . .]

Children by my bed who turn into rats that bite me. Big rats of an orange color with longish hair.

I meet some Rolling Stones, Mick Jagger and others, when they get off a bus. Outskirts of an American city. There is a deadly plague that seems to drive people insane and violent. It is moving in from rural areas to the cities. One of the pop group says he is going back to pick up some friends and then will return.

I say: "If you return."

Scene is now in NYC. I am on the Lower East Side and it looks like business as usual. I know that the plague hasn't hit yet, but will hit at any moment. Now I am trying to find my way back to my apartment, where I have some guns stashed. There are several people with me in-cluding, I think, Mick Jagger. I say: "Stay together and walk fast." Even the pavements and subways are falling apart and I can look down a

thousand feet into girders and rubble. The plague is everywhere now.
People are raving and stripping off their clothes. Corpses everywhere,
whether from the plague or violence I can't be sure. It is total Pande-
monium. [...]

Nightmare. In a dark room dressed in black. My face, however, is
clearly visible in white but no features can be made out. I think, Well,
I am safe. Then the mirror image, a full-length mirror, reaches out
black arms to me and I wake up groaning.

A tunnel which leads into a large round room with a domed top like
a truncated sphere. This is the womb, and as I approach the far corner I feel a strong magnetic pull, another few steps and I will not be
able to pull myself loose. I wrench free and move back to the tunnel
entrance. Here I meet Allen Ginsberg, who has a nosebleed. Now a cry
goes up: "THE DOGS THE DOGS!!"

And I realize that dogs have been released in the tunnel to force
us back into the womb. I look about for a means of escape. There is
some sort of scaffolding at the entrance to the tunnel. Could I hold myself off the ground? No, the dogs would get up and bite my fingers.

I see a technician ... a dental technician. Dr. ... forgot his name ...
but I recognize Charlie Kincaid. He will help me. We are waiting on
the Masks of Poseidon. These will protect us from the dogs so we can
walk back through the tunnel.

I am split into three people. One in a gray suit that I am occupying.
There is another, in a gray suit with wide shoulders, much younger ...
and a third, very young, in a sweater. I embrace him and ask if he is all
right. He says in a very weak voice: "Yes, I am all right."

Now his clothes are removed from the waist down. He has
undergone some sort of operation. There is what looks like a skinned
penis. Also another set of genitals. I am shocked and saddened and
begin to sob ... tears dripping down onto his mutilated body.

Orchestrate the singing.

Make a symphony of overlapping slow-down, speed-up singing.
Run singing backwards.

I am on the train. Can see the Hudson. The island. Get out of a boat.

198

Ruins of a red brick house . . . rubble and bricks and timbers . . . a bath-tub. Who lived here? The Visitors will meet me here. Walking around the island. Brush . . . trees . . . rocks . . . not much. About an acre, maybe less . . . switch to Lone Star Lake. Hiatus of calm. Snow everywhere. In front of the fireplace . . . now in the room dissolving in long gray empty roads and ditches . . . moving very fast now.

Met some aliens in the street and one of them gave me a pair of glasses. I am now in what looks like an optometrist's store, with mirrors and glass shelves, and find I can see everything quite clearly. The aliens form a group in Paris, and I am eating with them in a restaurant. They are not obvious aliens at first glance, but all rather out-landishly dressed in some sort of costumes, and one of them has a huge face, a foot across, on a normal-sized body. They seem to be well disposed. There are both men and women in the group. Now the bill comes, and I put in an amount that seems fair to me in some currency unknown to me. Large gray notes on parchment paper.

My Press Releaser Kim Carson said: "The only goal worth striving for is immortality." And fuck the physicists who say: "There is no picture with-out a frame. No life without death. Why, the only thing that gives life meaning and dignity is death. Why should there be another life? Don't you get enough here?" Indeed, yes: enough bullshit.

Now there are two routes to immortality. They might be desig-nated as: slow-down or speed-up, or straight-ahead or detour. Refer-ence aphorisms of the Old White Hunter. In the time that you face death directly, you are immortal. That's the straight-ahead route—take a little, leave a little, sure, skim a year off a thousand citizens, they won't know the difference—but what happens when you run short of citizens, which you will sooner or later? Also, speed-up route is a kill route, whereas slow-down is a manipulate, degrade, humiliate, enslave route.

So how does one face death head-on? . . . without flinching and without posturing—which is always to be seen as a form of evasion, worse than flinching, because covert. For the man who flinches and runs away, like Lord Jim and Francis Macomber, there is hope. But not for him who sticks out his chest and wraps himself in a flag, a Gal-lic shrug from the French naval officer in *Lord Jim,* one of the great characters of fiction:

"Parbleu, il s'en fuye, mais a laissé son cadavre en place . . ."
"He has run away, but left his carcass behind."
"Intrigué par ce cadavre?"
"Intrigued by that corpse?"
Not really . . . a well-known and documented schism, something familiar about that figure moving further and further away. "Why! Himself!" Like the song says, "They don't come back, won't come back, once they're gone . . ."

Black storm clouds cut by flashes of silver light, a green flash on the skyline. Glimpsed a sail in the distance, bright and clear for a moment, then wiped away by a veil of rain.

None of this happened, or rather it happened at the same time as the watches and meals and entries in the logbook, tomorrow and tomorrow of not seeing beyond the illusion of present time.

A painted ship, a painted ocean, a phantom crew going through the motions of watches, meals, entries, in the logbooks six miles off Santa Maria, simple men, plain pleasures. There was no security in the alligators. Where are you all going? *Quo vadis?* To Gnaoua, with alcohol to fortify their wines.

Like a young thief thinks he has a license to steal, a young writer thinks he has a license to write. You know what I mean right enough: riding along on it, it's coming faster than you can get it down and you know it's the real thing, you can't fake it, the writer has to have *been* there and make it back. Then it hits you, cold and heavy, like a cop's blackjack on a winter night: *Writer's Block.* Oh yes, he tried to warn me, the old hand, "You write too much, Bill . . ." I wouldn't listen.

Then it slugs you in the guts. For a whole year I couldn't remember my dreams. Tried going without pot and everything. It was like some gray bureaucrat wiped away the dream before my eyes as I tried to grasp one detail that would bring the dream back, the outlines: dead. James complained I sat for hours in my chair at the end of the loft, doing absolutely nothing. Stagnating without tranquillity. The pages and pages with nothing in them: the writer has been nowhere and brought nothing back. The false starts, the brief enthusiasm. Books that died for the lack of any reason to stay alive after ten pages. [. . .]

Don't want to write this. Have said no honest autobiography has ever been attempted, much less written, and no one could bear to read it. At this point I guess the reader thinks I am about to confess some juicy sex practices. Hardly. Guess I was twenty-four, working in the shop at Cobble Stone Gardens, which I hate to remember, when this Jew woman sent me around to the servants' entrance and I drove away clashing the gears and saying: *"Hitler is perfectly right!"* So you want it honest? You vant. You vant. You vant.

Back through the Sixties, slow letup in drug pressure...now back through the Fifties...Anslinger in full swing. Morphine and Dilaudid scripts...Pantopon Rose...Old-time junkies at 103rd and Broadway ...Back back clickety clack...Syrettes...World War II...The Thirties... Heroin is $28 an ounce—back back...the Crash, the Twenties...film stars on junk, Wally Reid...Wilson Mizner...World War I...Keep the home fires burning though the hearts are yearning...back before the laws...another air...a different light...free lunch and beer at five cents a mug...back...no lines to the present...cut all lines...here come the lamplighters, ghostly private places...Westmoreland Place ...Portland Place...empty houses, leaves blowing and drifting like shreds of time...radio silence on Portland Place...furtive seedy figures, rooming houses and chili parlors, hop joints, cathouses...

A road cut through heavy second-growth timber, the road structured from split logs, split side down, nailed to a framework. Looking north, the trees are flush with the road on the left side, and seem to have been shaved with an axe. Ahead there is a clearing. Location is northern Canada, Alaska, Siberia; there is a lake ahead. It is raining and there is water in puddles beside the road and ahead of us.

I am in a car and my father is driving. I seem to be lying down with my head behind my father's shoulders. Such roads, slicked over with wet clay, are slippery as greased glass, and I say from the back seat:

"DAD! *Please* slow down!"

Dream years ago: in a car, pinwheeling off the road, and I am out of my body with no pain, floating above the wreck.

From *Nip the Buds, Shoot the Kids*

The following passage is excerpted from the forthcoming translation of Kenzaburo Oe's first novel Nip the Buds, Shoot the Kids *(Marion Boyars, New York). First published in Japan in 1958 when Oe was 23, the novel tells the story of fifteen teenage reformatory boys evacuated to a remote mountain village in wartime. When a plague breaks out, the villagers blockade them there with a female evacuee.*

I went out on the road, which was bright under the moon. The fog was flowing, harsh and chill. The girl followed me outside, but I didn't look back. I didn't even know whether I could reach the other side of the valley or not. But in any case I wanted to hand over the girl, whose little face was wet with tears and whose whole body stank, to the bunch on the other side. I couldn't bear it.

As I came out of the forest, the trolley track, dripping from the fog, shone in the moonlight. Then the black looming mass of the barricade. The light in the hut on the far side where the guard should have been keeping watch had been put out. I turned back and spoke to the girl who was biting lips that were blue with cold.

"Wait here; I'll talk to them about you."

When I stepped onto the track's sleepers, taking care not to slip, the fog and a sharp chill came blowing up from beneath them, striking my cheeks and stinging my nostrils. Far below, the water current shining in the moonlight and the sound of it gnawing the rock made a swirling motion. Slowly, bent over like a beast, I went on walking over the sleepers. My excitement soon subsided. I thought what I was doing was quite trivial. But I had no intention of going back. So I half-closed my eyes to keep them from being hurt by the hard bitter wind and fixed all my attention on stepping on the dead center of each sleeper.

The track was very long and the wind was fierce. By the time I reached the barricade, piled with tree stumps, bundles of branches, boards, and chunks of rock, I was so tired that I wanted to lie down and sleep, and my throat was dry. I established that the barricade was too heavy and complicated for me to remove, but that if I climbed over it, it would collapse immediately. I peered at the underside of the sleepers. There was no other way. First I straightened up and put my frozen hands inside my trousers and in my groin to warm them. As my fingers gradually recovered their senses, they felt the presence of my penis, shrunken and wrinkled with cold and fear.

Placing my elbows on the sleepers, I curled up and slid my lower limbs through the narrow gap. The next moment, I was hanging from the sleepers by both hands, exposing my whole body in the valley's chill void. The harsh wind and cold, and a terrible loneliness, assailed me. I had to fight them. Twisting my body haphazardly like a shrimp simmering in tepid water, I swung from one sleeper to the next.

My strength almost exhausted, I put my hands on the last sleeper and, with a gasp that was almost a scream, chinned up, put my elbows on its upper surface which was covered with crystalline frost, and lifted my body up. I stretched out on top of the sleepers and breathed heavily. But I couldn't lie there in full view in the moonlight. If I was shot at from the guard hut, my head would be smashed by the first bullet. Exhaling harsh gasps, I walked over the sleepers for the last short distance and when I reached firm ground I ran up the slope beside the dark shrubs, staying out of the moonlight. Then, without even having to take the map from my breast pocket and look at it, I went through a sparse woodland of oaks and chestnuts planted together in a jumble, and there in front of me was a fairly small village, peaceful in the moonlight. It appeared suddenly, in the same way that every other farming community had appeared so far.

I went down the sloping road spotted with rounded pebbles and into the village. It was made up of houses, roadside trees, and convoluted alleys that were almost the same as those in the village where we were incarcerated. But there was a subtle difference in the air in this village, and that made me scared. People were living there. Strangers were living there. The village was quiet and I felt the stirring of domestic animals from the interiors, the dark cold interiors, of the houses. I went on walking between the low-eaved houses, casting a small shadow in the moonlight. The strangers who had cut us off and stood guard over us were sleeping in those houses. Fear and a violent surge of excitement made waves of trembling race over my frost-nipped skin. To suppress the urge to run away as fast as I could, I concentrated on searching for the doctor's house.

I knocked on the Western-style door of the doctor's house, which was fitted with pocked and bubbled panes of glass. Then, stepping back a pace, right into the moonlight, I watched the door with its glass panes, so rare in the village. A light went on behind it, a figure came up to the entrance, mumbling in its throat, and the small animal-like head of the doctor I had seen at the warehouse poked out from the slightly opened door. We eyed each other very warily. I thought in consternation that I must say something, but I was choked up and almost crying.

"Hey," said the doctor in a voice that made my limp feelings suddenly harden. "What have you come here for?"

I was silent, staring at him wide-eyed. His plump cheeks and small nose were filled with something like fear, and that hardened my heart still further.

"You, what have you come here for? If you get violent, I'll call someone."

"I won't get violent," I said in an excited, thickened voice, curbing my anger. "I didn't come here for that."

"What did you come for?" he repeated.

"The village girl was left behind in the warehouse. She wants to get out of the village. You, take her out, please."

The doctor looked me over searchingly. I saw his bared gums soaked and glistening with saliva, and cunning spread quickly from them all over his face. I repeated hastily:

"Please, come and do it."

"How many of you have contracted the disease? How many of you are left alive?" he asked.

"What?" I said in surprise. "We're not ill; the girl's fine too. There's no plague."

He looked at me more carefully.

"If you think I'm lying, take a look at me. I'll undress so you can examine me."

"Don't speak so loud," said the doctor. "Who said I'd take a look at you?"

I lowered my hand from the coat buttons which I had almost undone to bare my upper body in the moonlight. He wouldn't listen to me at all.

"You're a doctor, aren't you? It's your job to see if someone's ill or not, isn't it?"

"Don't be impudent," he said, suddenly showing anger. "Go back; don't come over to this side again."

"I thought you'd tell everyone that there's no plague going round us. You're a doctor," I said, flushed all over with indignation. "But you're sending me back?"

"Go back!" he said. "If the villagers find out, you'll pay for it. You'll get me into trouble. Go back!"

I squared my shoulders defiantly. The doctor came out in front of me from behind the door, wearing a stiff gown like an animal skin.

"Go back, don't come here again," he said, quickly twisting my arm and speaking in a voice filled with anger. Letting out a little groan from the pain, I struggled to break free from his strong grip, but he stood there firmly, immeasurably massive.

"If the villagers find you wandering around here, you won't survive," he said. "I'll make you go back."

His hand grabbed the scruff of my neck. I had to start walking, dragged along by him, not even able to squirm. I was burning with anger. But it was hard to release myself from that humiliating position. The doctor hurried me along, almost shoving me.

"You're disgusting; you're supposed to be a doctor and you won't try to help us," I said, my voice thin and high-pitched, squeezed out from my constricted throat.

The doctor's arm pressed harder, and I groaned with pain. I was dragged along like that. Finally I was thrown down in front of the trolley track. From the cold ground, I looked up at the doctor's stocky body, looming black against the background of the dark forest. It was filled with overwhelming strength and authority.

"You're just going to watch us die," I said. I felt very ashamed that my voice was so weak and fearful, but to lie there in silence would have been more shameful. "You're disgusting."

The doctor bent down, and a terrific impact struck my back as though I had been hit by a heavy stone. I cried out and writhed away, rolling over to avoid his foot, drawn back for the next kick. Vindictively, he tried to pursue me. Screaming with fear, I crawled down to the trolley track and went out along it.

I was completely exhausted. But when I saw the doctor bend down to pick up a stone to throw at me, I knew I couldn't stay there. I crawled along the track, clawing at the sleepers with panicky fingers, then when I reached the barricade I slid my legs, trembling with rage in that ignoble position, underneath the track.

When I lifted my body up onto the trolley track again after the arduous struggle, using almost all the strength that I had left to do a last chin-up, I could only pant violently, my chest rising and falling like a tormented beast. Then I was mad with a desperate fury. My fingertips were wounded and bleeding. I thought I heard someone's footsteps receding behind me, but instead of turning round, I gazed at the end of the long track illuminated by the moon. The girl was looking at me, her small head peeping out from behind the winch apparatus.

I stood up and walked over along the sleepers, forcing my wobbly knees into action. When my feet touched the other side, the earth on that side where we were definitely shut in, the girl jumped out, staring at me with wide-open eyes that shone like those of a feverish child. We stared at each other like that for a long time. Anger raged over my body. Breathing hard, I tore myself free from her pressing, entangling gaze and started to walk. She followed me hastily, but I went on walking briskly without slackening my pace.

Those pigs, those bloody pigs, I shouted to myself as I walked. The scruff of my neck tingled with pain where I had been grabbed. The doctor's baseness, his bestial strength and my weakness. I couldn't do anything about those pigs. I quickened my pace to prevent my helpless indignation and my sorrow from mingling with my rage. Now the girl was trotting and panting. As she panted, she went on mumbling something over and over again, but I didn't even try to catch it.

We passed through the forest, went down the paved road that was bright in the moonlight, passed between the houses where our sleeping comrades lay and came out in front of the girl's warehouse. She stopped and I stopped. Then we stared at each other again. Tears had gathered in her swollen, bloodshot eyes and they reflected the moonlight, sparkling. Now her thin lips were moving without emitting a sound. Suddenly the meaning of the words they had been repeating became clear to me.

I thought you wouldn't come back, they said over and over again. I thought you wouldn't come back. They cried out the words, mingled with senseless convulsive spasms. I turned my eyes away from her lips and looked down at my sore fingers. The blood was dripping on the paving stones. Suddenly the girl's hand reached out, then she bent down and took my fingers between her lips, and her hard tongue, moving in little darts, touched my wounds repeatedly and moistened them with sticky saliva. The nape of her neck, rounded and pliant as a pigeon's back, was moving slightly under my bowed head.

A feeling swelled up inside me, then suddenly ballooned and went right to my head. I grabbed the girl's shoulders roughly and pulled her up. I no longer saw the expression on her small upturned face. I hugged her like a cornered, panicky chicken and ran with her into the darkened warehouse.

We went straight into the completely dark interior, and I silently dropped my trousers and lifted her skirt: I threw myself down on the girl's body. I groaned as my erect penis, like an asparagus stalk, caught in my underpants and was almost bent double. Then contact with the cold, dry, papery, flurried surface of her sex, and withdrawal with little shivers. I sighed deeply.

That was all. I stood up and put on my trousers, fumbling, then went outside, leaving the girl lying there breathing unsteadily. Outdoors, the cold was swiftly deepening and the moonlight poured its mineral hardness down on the trees and paving stones. I was still madly angry and frenzied mutterings filled my mouth, but a rich sensation filled with sweetness slowly raised its head from beneath all that. As I ran up the slope my eyes filled with tears and I tensed my facial muscles to stop them overflowing down my cheeks.

Translated from the Japanese by Paul St. John Mackintosh
and Maki Sugiyama

Kenzaburo Oe.

From *Wave Patterns: A Dialogue*

The following dialogue is excerpted from the transcript of a conversation between Kenzaburo Oe and Kazuo Ishiguro, author of The Remains of the Day *and* An Artist of the Floating World, *that took place in November of 1989—on the occasion of Ishiguro's first return visit to Japan (sponsored by the Japan Foundation) since he had left thirty years earlier at the age of five. A longer version of this interview was published in* Grand Street 38 *in 1991.*

KENZABURO OE: In my book *The Silent Cry*, I wrote about Shikoku. I was born and grew up in a mountain village on that island. When I was eighteen, I went to the University of Tokyo to study French literature. As a result, I found myself completely cut off from my village, both culturally and geographically. Around that time my grandmother died, and my mother was getting older. The legends and traditions and folklore of my village were being lost. Meanwhile, here I was in Tokyo, imagining and trying to remember those things. The act of trying to remember and the act of creating began to overlap. And that is the reason I began to write novels. I tried to write them using the methods of French literature that I had studied. Reading your novels, and thinking about English literary history, I get the strong impression that, in terms of method, you are a novelist at the very forefront of English literature.

KAZUO ISHIGURO: That's very flattering. I'm very interested to hear some of the background about your being cut off from your past in Shikoku. Are you saying that the urge to remember or stay in touch with your past was actually crucial in making you become a writer?

KO: I have a book that is just coming out in French translation from Gallimard, *M/T et l'histoire des merveilles de la forêt*. The "M" is for matriarch and the "T" is for trickster. A while ago I wrote a book called *Contemporary Games*, about the myths of the village and the universe of the village. As I wrote *M/T et l'histoire*, I listened once more to my grandmother talking about cosmology, and wrote it down just as it was, in her own words. In fact, the history of my village is already lost. Almost everyone has forgotten it. For example, there is a place where dozens of people were killed in a riot, but no one remembers that. My family and especially my grandmother remembered those things very well, and told me about them. I grew up in the village listening to these stories. Then, when I was fourteen, I moved to the city and was completely cut off while they were all dying. So now the only person who remembers the core of the myths of that village is me. This is what I want to write about now. I want to write a book that will sum up or finish all of my work up to now. These things will be the main theme of the book, and right now they are what is most important to me.

KI: I hope the English translation will be appearing very shortly. I look forward very much to reading it. I think *The Silent Cry* is an extraordinary work. One of the reasons I think it's such a special work is that it's often difficult for a writer to get a certain distance from very personal events in his life that have touched and disturbed him. This book seems to stem from such an event, but at the same time you seem to have kept control, to have maintained an artistic discipline, so that it actually becomes a work of art that has meaning for everybody. It's not simply about Mr. Oe. It strikes me that one of the ways in which you manage that is a certain kind of humor, a unique tone. It's very different from the kind of humor found in most of Western literature, which is mainly based on jokes. In your books, everything has a peculiar sense of humor that is always on the verge of tragedy—a very dark humor. This is one of the ways in which you seem to have been able to keep under control events that must be very close to you. Mr. Oe the artist has always managed to keep in control of the work. But do you think this sort of humor is something unique to your own writing, or have you gotten it from a larger Japanese tradition?

KO: It's interesting that you should ask that, because one of the things I feel is unique about your work is your control over the distance from the periods and characters in your work. All of your books have a distinct tone, even though they are connected on a deeper level. So I appreciate your comments about the tone and distance in my works.

I think that the problem of humor, which you just brought up, is a very important one. This is one of the points in which I differ from Yukio Mishima. Mishima was very strongly rooted in the traditions of Japanese literature, especially the traditions of the center—Tokyo or Kyoto—urban traditions. I come from a more peripheral tradition, that of a very provincial corner of the island of Shikoku. It's an extremely strange place, with a long history of maltreatment, out there beyond the reach of culture. I think my humor is the humor of the people who live in that place. Mishima had a great deal of confidence in his humor; perhaps it's accurate to say that his was the humor of the center, whereas mine is the humor of the periphery.

KI: I would be quite interested to hear what you feel about Mishima. I'm often asked about Mishima in England—all the time—by journalists. They expect me to be an authority on Mishima because of my Japanese background. Mishima is very well known in England, and in the West generally, largely because of the way he died. But also I suspect that Mishima's image confirms certain stereotypical images of Japanese people for the West. And this is partly why I think he is easy for Western audiences. He fits certain characteristics. Of course, committing *seppuku* is one of the clichés. He was politically very extreme. The problem is that the whole image of Mishima in the West hasn't helped people there form an intelligent approach to Japanese culture and Japanese people. It has perhaps helped people to remain locked in certain prejudices and very superficial, stereotypical images of what Japanese people are like.

KO: The observations you just made about the reception of Mishima in Europe are accurate. Mishima's entire life, certainly including his death by *seppuku*, was a kind of performance designed to present the image of an archetypal Japanese. Moreover, this image was not the kind that arises spontaneously from a Japanese mentality. It was the superficial image of a Japanese as seen from a European point of view, a fantasy. Mishima acted out that image just as it was. He created himself exactly in accordance with it. That was the way he lived, and that was the way he died. Professor Edward Said uses the word "orientalism" to refer to the impression that Europeans have of the Orient. He insists that orientalism is a view held by Europeans and has nothing to do with the people who actually live in the Orient. But Mishima thought the opposite. He said, in effect, "Your image of the Japanese is me." I think he wanted to show something by living and dying in exact accordance with the image. That was the kind of man he was and that was why he gained literary glory in Europe and the world.

But what in fact happened is that Mishima presented a false image. As a result, the conception of Japanese people held by Europeans has Mishima at one pole and people like Akio Morita, chairman of Sony, at the other pole. In my opinion, both poles are inaccurate. But if this is the case, where can we look for a more accurate image of the Japanese people? [In] your book *An Artist of the Floating World*, at the very end there is a scene with a number of young Japanese and the artist, who is looking at them in a warmhearted way. I think that people like those young Japanese really do live in Japan, and that they are the ones who have brought prosperity to the Japanese economy. Of course, Mishima had nothing to say about them. And writers like me, who take a negative view of Japan, have not captured them either. So I think that your novel exerted a good influence on perceptions of Japan in Europe, a kind of antidote to the image of Mishima.

The Japanese themselves want to be perceived as peaceful and gentle, like Japanese art—landscape paintings and so on. They don't want to be seen as economic imperialists or military invaders. They would like others to think of flower paintings, something quiet and beautiful, when they think of Japan. When your books first began to appear in Japan, that was how they were introduced. You were described as a very quiet and peaceful author, and therefore a very Japanese author. But from the first I doubted that. I felt that this was an author with a tough intelligence. And in fact that has been demonstrated again with each of your books. Your style always involves a double structure, with two or more intertwined elements. I also felt that this kind of strength was not very Japanese, that this person was, rather, from England.

KI: Well, I don't try to be a quiet writer. That's really a question of technique more than anything else. There's a surface quietness to my books—there aren't a lot of people getting murdered or anything like that. But for me they're not quiet books, because they're books that deal with the things that disturb me the most and the questions that worry me the most. They're anything but quiet to me.

I wonder, Mr. Oe, do you feel responsible for how Japanese people are perceived abroad? When you are writing your books, are you conscious of an international audience and of what the books will do to Western people's perceptions of Japan? Or do you not think about things like that?

KO: I was interviewed once by a German television station. The interviewer had translated one of my books into German. He asked me whether it was very important to me to be translated into German. I said no, and a deathly silence fell over the studio. The reason I said no is simply that I write my books for Japanese readers rather than for foreigners. Moreover, the Japanese readers I have in mind are a limited group. The people I write for are people of my own generation, people who have had the same experiences as myself. So when I go abroad, or am translated abroad or criticized abroad, I feel rather indifferent about it. The responsibilities I feel are to Japanese readers, people who are living together with me in this environment.

Speaking as a reader, foreign literature is very important to me. William Blake is important to me. I've written one book based on Blake, and one based on Malcolm Lowry. Another book was about a Dante specialist who lives out in the country. With

respect to Dante, I have been influenced in various ways by scholars from your country. So in that sense I have been much influenced by foreign literature. I read your books in English, for
example. Still, I think that when I write my books, I write them for
Japanese readers. I feel a certain sense of responsibility that I just
can't break out of, even though I feel that there is probably something mistaken about that attitude. Naturally, I believe that a real
novelist is international, like yourself. In your case, of course, I
think that in addition to being international you are also very
English. In *The Remains of the Day* you discovered viewpoints from
which it is possible to describe both English people and Americans
well. The viewpoint is completely different from that of a Japanese person or a Chinese person. It might be that I am a more
Japanese author than Mishima. I myself hope that younger Japanese authors will be able to discover a more international stand-
point or outlook.

KI: There never seems to be a clear relationship between the audience an author thinks he is addressing and the audience that in
fact the author does come to address. Many of the great classical
writers, whether the ancient Greeks or whoever, had no idea they
would eventually address people from cultures very, very different
from their own. Possibly Plato was writing simply for the people
who were living in Athens at the time, but of course we read him
many, many years later in very different cultures. I sometimes
worry that writers who are conscious of addressing an international audience could actually have quite a reverse effect, that
something very important in literature might actually die because
people are watering down their artistic instincts. It's almost like a
mass-marketing exercise.

I worry particularly because this is a time when American culture, or what you might call Anglo-American culture, has become
pervasive all around the world—in Asia, Latin America, and so
forth. It seems to be growing and growing. Perhaps it is very important that writers not worry about this question of audience.
You yourself, Mr. Oe, may think you are writing only for your own
generation, for the Japanese. But your books are read by lots of
people outside that group. People want to translate your work. It
seems that as the years go by your reputation grows in different

parts of the world. This shows that someone can address a small group of people, but if that work is powerful and sincere it will have a universal, international audience.

On the other hand, I know that there are many writers who are consciously trying to write the novel that is all ready for translation. And of course nobody particularly wants to read these things, because they have lost some sort of initial strength that comes from the intensity of addressing a small group. Perhaps whether a writer is international or not is something that the writer cannot control. It's almost accidental. But often, I think, the deeper the work, and the deeper the truth of the work, the more likely it is to be international, whether the author is consciously addressing a small group of people or a large number of people. Do you think younger writers in Japan are worried about this question of how international they are?

KO: In last evening's edition of the *Asahi Shimbun* [one of Japan's major newspapers] there was an article about how a translation of a work by the novelist Haruki Murakami is being read widely in New York. The article quoted a review in the *New York Times* to the effect that it was now possible to imagine a literature of the Pacific Rim.

For the past week I have been thinking about just what sort of novelist you are. My conclusion is that, rather than being an English author or a European author, you are an author who writes in English. In terms of furnishing the materials for literature, there is a tremendous power in the English language. Somehow it seems that the initiative in world literature has been with English, especially in the field of the novel. As long as he has the English language, an author can leave England and still remain a great writer. Lawrence was that way, and Lawrence Durrell; also E. M. Forster. I felt that by thinking of you in this way, as a writer of English, I had got hold of something essential. By way of comparison, Murakami writes in Japanese, but his writing is not really Japanese. If you translate it into American English it can be read very naturally in New York. I suspect that this sort of style is not really Japanese literature, nor is it really English literature. But as a matter of fact, a young Japanese author is being read widely in the United States, and I think that this is a good sign for the future of Japanese culture. A young Japanese writer has achieved something that I was never able to achieve, nor Mishima nor Kōbō Abe.

KI: I think I too share these same worries. I attended a lecture by the European intellectual George Steiner, who is at Cambridge and very well known in Britain. I think you are familiar with many of his ideas. One of his constant worries is that all the cultures of the world are disappearing because they are being swallowed up by this ever-growing large blanket called Anglo-American culture. He is very disturbed by the fact that scientific papers in China and here in Japan are often written originally in English because they have to be presented at conferences where only English is understood. In communist countries the young people listen to the latest Western rock music. He is very afraid of a certain kind of death of culture, because this bland, colorless, huge blanket called Anglo-Americanism is spreading around the world. In order to survive, people have to sacrifice many of the things that make their culture unique and in fact make their art and culture mean something, and instead contribute to this strange thing that is conquering the world.

I think that is quite an important thing to be concerned about. Certainly my generation of writers in Britain has perhaps not worried about that kind of thing enough. We have perhaps been concerned about the opposite problem, of not being international enough. I think this is certainly a problem that we have to think about. I think it will be very strange if we all contribute to the same sort of culture, if we're all addressing the same sort of audience. We could all end up like international television. A lot of television programs now are rather superficial, but they're international. It would be sad if literature and serious art were to go the same way—to the lowest common denominator—in order to appear international.

There is a sense among younger writers in England that England is not an important country anymore. The older generation of writers assumed that Britain was a very important country, and so if you wrote about Britain and British problems it would automatically be of global significance. The younger generation of writers in England is very aware of the fact that this is no longer true, that England is now rather like a little provincial town in the world. Some younger British writers have a kind of inferiority

Kenzaburo Oe.

complex; that is, they have to consciously make an effort to address international themes, because if they simply write about life in Britain, nobody is going to be interested. Perhaps that feeling doesn't exist in the United States or Japan, since there is a strong sense that these two societies are now at the center of the world, and that they are somehow going to dominate the twenty-first century. But, certainly, living in England, I feel that same pressure to be international. Otherwise I'm going to end up in the same position as Danish or Swedish writers, of being very peripheral, because a lot of the great questions of today are passing Britain by. In a way, I think young Japanese authors don't need to feel that sort of inferiority, just because of the way history is moving.

KO: Of course, I have nothing against the fact that Japan is becoming rich because of radios and automobiles. But I do think that the state of the economy and the state of literature are unrelated. I think Japanese authors should clearly realize that Japanese literature is very peripheral. When a peripheral literature attempts to become a central literature, one of the things that happens is that it tries to become exotic. I think Mishima tried to create a literature of the exotic. But I believe that attempt was mistaken. Paradoxically, it may be possible for Japanese writers to play a certain role in world literature if they express Japanese concerns in a literature of the periphery.

I am familiar with George Steiner. He seems to be very fond of the idea that things are dying—first it was tragedy and now it is culture. I think that the image of Anglo-American culture as a huge blanket spreading across the world is one of his best. But I can't really agree with what you said about England being a peripheral nation in terms of the world economy and international relations. I believe that in terms of culture, England still occupies a very important place in the world, and will continue to do so in the future. Looking forward to the twenty-first century, it doesn't seem to me that Japan will become a cultural center just because of its economic strength. I don't believe that American cultural spokesmen will have a very great deal of power, or that Soviet cultural spokesmen will be very powerful. I think that in the twenty-first century, statements by isolated writers and scholars from small countries that appear to be on the periphery will play a very important role in world culture. One example is the novelist Italo Calvino, who recently died a tragic death. He was scheduled to deliver the Mellon Lectures at Harvard University, and was working on the manuscript for those lectures until he died, on the day before he was due to leave for the United States. The manuscript has been translated into English as *Six Memos for the Next Millenium*. Reading it, I think that this work by a novelist from Italy, a country that is economically and politically on the periphery, contains things that will be of central importance in the next century. Another example is the Czech novelist Milan Kundera, now living in exile in France. Reading, for example, the Israel Address, which is found at the end of his book *The Art of the Novel*, I think we will find the most central expression of how a writer will have to live and act today. So I think what writers from Japan must learn is that they need to think about how they can contribute to world culture as representatives of a small but cultured nation in Asia. Moreover, they should do so without the help of businessmen or politicians. They will have to open up on their own a road to England, or a road to France, simply as writers.

KI: I would like to add to my earlier remarks. It wasn't simply because Britain was declining as an economic power that I was suggesting that writers in Britain had a sense they were peripheral. I don't think it is really so much in connection with economic power. In fact, I think it is in some ways quite the reverse.

Writers from Britain, and to a certain extent writers from Germany and France—and I myself have had this experience— go to international writers' conferences and somehow feel inferior compared to writers who come from places like Africa or Eastern Europe or Latin America, in the sense that in many of the great intellectual battles—between liberty and authoritarian regimes, or between communism and capitalism, or between the Third World and the industrialized world—the front line somehow seems to be in these countries, and there seems to be a more clearly defined role for writers like Kundera or some of the African writers. Writers from all the Eastern European countries always seem to have some sort of clear political role to play. This may well be a mistaken assumption, but it's an easy assumption that comes over a lot of us who come from the safer countries, if you like, the safe, prosperous countries like Britain or West Germany or France, although the situation has suddenly changed for the West Germans.

Perhaps it's a good thing that British writers feel they have to travel, at least in their imaginations. I think the younger generation of British writers, much more than the older generation, tends to write novels that are not set in Britain, or at least not set in their time. They look back through history for a time when Britain itself was in crisis, and so the war figures quite large. Or they use their imaginations to create complete imaginary landscapes. This kind of thing is happening more and more, and I think it comes out of the idea that somehow England is far away from the important events—political and social—in the world. Perhaps writers in Japan and the United States do not feel it quite so much, because there is a sense that somehow, quite aside from the economic question, Japan and America are at the forefront of something crucial that is about to happen in the world. I think that has a certain effect on how writers view their work and on where they go for material to feed their imaginations.

KO: When I myself go abroad to participate in various conferences, it is always simply as an individual writer. I think that the things I have talked about have been more or less unrelated to Japan's economic growth. My sense of Japan is that it is still a peripheral country, and that in spite of its economic power it still does not live up to its international role, particularly in Asia. Thinking back, I think I may share some of the responsibility for this state of affairs, so I talk about that and the sort of things that a writer, as a writer, might be able to do to compensate.

For some reason, Japanese writers tend to stay away from international writers' conferences. Up to now, at least, there have not been many authors who have gone abroad to speak out about Japan's place in the world, about the contradictions felt by Japanese writers in the midst of economic prosperity, about the things that trouble them deeply. So for my part I am trying to do that, little by little. Japan has many very capable businessmen and politicians, but as a novelist I want to speak out internationally about things that they never mention. And I think it is meaningful for writers from abroad, especially young writers like yourself, to come to Japan

to look closely at this country and to meet Japanese intellectuals. I
hope this will lead to a deeper understanding of things such as the
difficult role played by Japanese intellectuals amid material prosperity, and to cultural encounters at a genuinely substantial level.

In Praise of the Death of a Child

You have been over-educated.
When the grass holds its fingers, you no longer count,
You know gray bird sky.

And that quaint cock of your headstone
Tilts the shivering wind
Deliberately. You are not so innocent.

Mourning has set you in stone
And white weeds breathe
When you twist in the earth.

The Late Foxes

Blue veins of sky
Nourish the china clouds.
Evening is so far away and empty,
The fields are subdued
And hand out silence.

Only the white, informative flowers
Pulling a skin of light upon themselves,
Catch on a shred of evening
And drag her dull blue hood across the fields.

Now they come. Like orange ghosts
Barely parting the air. The wind of a paw,
A whistle of leaves.
The hedge is pregnant with orange shapes
That walk like water.

Fox breath peels off in a rind of fear.
Everything they see is an emergency.
Our own two sullen shapes
Are radar squeaking across the fields.
And we are lucid with danger.

Hold. They stand in a last spadeful of light.
Suddenly red and present. Still as a tomb.
Noses cocked to the air. Then they are not.
A helter-skelter of dark shapes
Bumbling across the fields.

And we are left, time spilling about us.
The hedges catching dribbles of early moon.
We are late foxes now
Creeping about our business on a surly night.

LOUISE LAWLER

A PART OF THE PICTURE

MAD GARDE

A Part of the Picture

Louise Lawler's photographs of art in situ show us the unshown, art from private collections, in auction houses or office areas—art which is private or available to a select few, only potentially visible. In these diverse social spaces she discovers paintings, sculpture, and furniture which, arranged in their various configurations, have become precious, commodified objects and decorative elements. In her photograph *What Goes On Here*, we glimpse a prominent New York art dealer's home, a hallway precisely arranged with two small Andy Warhol portraits and a Roy Lichtenstein furniture work. The setting is as much the subject of the photograph as is the art—in this orderly passageway, art becomes not a commercial commodity but part of a home, a manifestation of personal selection and involvement. The same holds true for *Overlooking Central Park*, where a Jasper Johns painting hangs on a sliver of wall, between two shade-drawn windows, over an immaculate desk. Here we focus on the placement and display of the artwork, which is unglamorous and confined. In *To Scale*, Frank Stella's wall relief, hanging at the entrance to the advertising agency Saatchi & Saatchi, is seen from outside through the lobby's revolving doors. More than a work of art on display, it is also a dramatic sign of privilege and wealth. The home and work environments that Lawler shows us are curiously unpopulated, yet one can imagine their inhabitants with little difficulty. The viewer becomes voyeur, piecing together others' lives through clues in the vernacular of style. By showing us art that is bound to its context, dependent on its environment, Lawler exposes and destabilizes the conventions of domesticity, politeness, and comfort in art.

—Peter Doroshenko

Bringing It All Back Home

"He was the best radical reporter and writer of his time, the most grace-ful stylist and, spiritually, the person least amenable to conformity I've ever met. If it's ever needed it, he gave extremism a good name."
Alexander Cockburn

The following is drawn from conversations between Andrew Kopkind and Jean Stein, 1987–1994.

I started working at *Time* when I was 26. And, in 1961, it was one of the best jobs that you could get in American journal-ism. They gave me what I thought was a lot of money for those days, plus you could bank it. That was the line they told you the minute you got out there to the Los Angeles Bureau: Bank your salary. The other great line was: Put it down as a lunch. I'd fly to Aspen for a week and put it down as a lunch. A couple of times I was brought into the bureau chief's office and told that my expense account was too low. There was nothing terribly evil about it, it was just corrupt. It was an old-boys' network, it was all Ivy League, it was all friends.

I was assigned to San Francisco for a year in the fall of 1964. I was right across the bay from the University of California, Berkeley, where the Free Speech Movement was starting to really rev up. The antiwar protests were beginning, and the students were being hassled by the administration. By rights I should have been very much involved in this thing, as a reporter and as a politically in-terested person. But I was very alienated from it, and I didn't know why. And then I realized that it had to do with working for

Time, and not being able to express anything in an honest or authentic way. The whole culture of *Time* was so antistudent and anti-Black and anti-Beatnik, and that's what produced the culture of the alienated *Time* correspondent, the detachment, the cynicism.

And it was strange because six months later, Berkeley was one of the biggest things in my life. I was working for *The New Republic* and doing a different kind of journalism, and I got really involved in all the movements I had avoided. I think that was key to the '60s: if you were in an institution that somehow protected you from expressing yourself, you couldn't make a commitment of any kind—in fact, just the opposite. And the defense against that was to ascribe to the '50s values of intellectualism and cynicism, the historical and political analysis that could analyze anything away. Even if you were sympathetic, you'd say, "oh, it's not going to amount to anything," or "these people are stupid," or "they're immature," or "they're acting out against their parents," or da-te-da-da-da. Or "they're middle class." There were a million ways for our generation to delegitimize any kind of commitment.

But then I worked for *The New Republic* and suddenly had the possibility of becoming a political actor. I had never been to the South to report before and I didn't know anything about it. I got to Atlanta first and I met Pat Watters, an ex-newspaperman, through someone at *The New Republic*. We had a drink or three and he told me what was going on and suggested that I meet with Julian Bond, whose name I didn't know at that point. I called the SNCC* office, and I got Julian. He met me at a coffee shop that everybody went to, a huge garish, modern, coffee shop, and we talked for hours and hours that first night I was in Atlanta, and he told me all about the Civil Rights movement, about the radical analysis, strategy, and sensibility. It was the first time that I had really heard this and it just made perfect sense to me. Then he told me when I got over to Alabama to speak to a couple of people, one of whom was Ivanhoe Donaldson. So I went over to Selma the next day, and Stokely Carmichael was there and Cleve Sellers, and that first very intelligent, educated, middle-class, if you will, Howard University collection of people who were good at talking to whites of their generation on the verge of liberal radical conversion.

---

* Student Nonviolent Coordinating Committee

I was there for virtually the whole event over the course of three or four weeks, with rallies building up to the march. Then the march made a false start one day. It was the day that Martin Luther King was supposed to come, but it was decided strategically that he shouldn't. Andy Young came and more or less dissembled—if you can put it that way—telling us that Dr. King was detained on urgent business in Atlanta. John Lewis was sent into the fray where he was beaten mercilessly. He has never recovered, and his speech is still slurred. We suddenly realized that the whole thing was a setup when we went over the bridge and came back again. I saw all the strategic stuff going on, and what the role of SNCC was—to be the shock troops, struggling for the control and definition of the Black movement.

Then I got back and wrote a big piece about SNCC in *The New Republic.* It was the first major piece about the radical Civil Rights movement in the context of the larger Civil Rights movement, written for a national liberal audience. It was impressionistic, but it included political analysis. It got a lot of comment because this hadn't been formulated before. I got very excited. I remember talking to Arthur Waskow at the Institute for Policy Studies, and I said, "Arthur, are there any people up north doing this?" And he said, "Well, as a matter of fact, yes, it's called Students for a Democratic Society—they have this Economic Research and Action Project, organizing projects in the slums of ten or fifteen cities." And I said, "Gee, I think I'll do that. Community organizing sounds great." It sounds funny now, but the vocabulary and the ideas were, to most people, completely new then. I had never read Saul Alinksy; I didn't have a background in any of this. So Arthur said, "Well, you might go to two or three places."

That was in the spring of '65 and the genie was out of the bottle. I wound up in Chicago, where it was a matter of organizing tough white hillbillies, usually immigrants from Appalachia, and the people there included Rennie Davis and Todd Gitlin. Then I went to Cleveland, and there were Carol McEldowney and Paul Potter and Sharon Jeffrey. The next year Kathy Boudin came, and Billy Ayers and Terry Robbins, the whole crowd. Then I went to Newark where Tom Hayden and Connie Brown were. And then I came back and did a big piece about SDS. This was a whole world that had opened up to me and not only was I writing about it, I was really thinking that it was terribly important. When you feel you have discovered something, a lot of creative energy goes into writing about it. And that was my first entry into the world of real heated political debate on the left.

The piece was a great success, and I started to chronicle over the course of several years what was going on with all these people. I was always one of the first stops when everyone came to Washington, and everyone was always coming for one thing or another, to get money, or to go to a march, or to picket, or to lobby, or throw rocks at bank windows. One of the things I remember most about the '60s is that for years my rug in Washington was absolutely full of tear gas. People would wear army jackets which would get saturated with it and they'd come to the house, throw their jackets on the floor and the tear gas would get into the rug. It isn't actually a gas—apparently they're molecules that have a little hook in them. They get in your rug and you can't get them out. And the rug was unwashable. I would go to the supermarket across the street and get these rug-cleaning devices to try to get it out. And of course people would always hang out on the rug— they hung out on the floor all the time in those days; no one had furniture. Everyone would be sneezing and crying, and there hadn't been a demonstration for months!

But I remember a conversation with Todd Gitlin and Carol McEldowney and some SDS people who were concerned about what was happening—which was that I was, in fact, defining what the movement was. It bothered them and it bothered me too, because it was like something was happening to the movement. It was being defined in this kind of national left liberal political consciousness by *The New Republic* and this was the mediation of these people's experience. They wanted recognition and they wanted legitimacy, so they were certainly interested in having someone write about them who was sympathetic. On the other hand, when anything is mediated, it is removed from reality, so it is of course not reality—it is media.

This was the greatest tension in my own life all through the '60s. What I ultimately could not deal with was my inability to feel authentic in any role. I remember hating having to write about what I was doing, but on the other hand not wanting to do it unless I was writing about it. Savoring my position on the margins of all this, but also finding it existentially frustrating. You can't really do something and make sense of it at the same time. This responsibility freaked me out increasingly over the years. And eventually, in 1970, it made me stop writing. I couldn't figure out who I was, and what I was doing this for, and the movement seemed to have gone completely out of control and disappeared into a million crazy bits.

But of all the places I went and the things I did in that early period, the most wrenching, devastating, and enlightening experience was in the SDS house in Cleveland. There were a lot of wonderful people there, one of whom was Carol McEldowney, who was this sort of Swedish ivy plant that we're still trying to clone sixteen years later. They were organizing a community called "The West Side," which was really scruffy. It was worse than down at the heels, it was ground at the heels... white homeless people and welfare mothers. There was no community, there were highways intersecting it and it was so depressing. The worst of the rust belt. They had rented a rickety old wooden-frame house. And Carol took a whole week to walk around the inner city and talk to me about it. It was an amazing week. She and I walked up to these scenes of urban desolation over the Cuyahoga River, which was on fire. It was the first time I'd seen a river burning—from the oil pollution and chemicals. It looked like some sort of Tolkienian harbor, desolate, postnuclear.

I became really emotionally involved with this whole experience. At the same time, I had a very good friend from college, Dan Silverberg, who had married and lived in Cleveland and was in investments or something. He was a happy-go-lucky guy. He had been my idea of what Cleveland was. I called him and he said, "Come out to my country club for dinner." The whole thing seemed so horrible to me. We couldn't make an arrangement until late in the week, and by that time I was going through what R. D. Laing calls an ontological break. I was becoming radicalized, but I didn't know it then. I couldn't put a name on it. I was in a period of high excitement, but was trying to be calm about it. I was a reporter, I had on my reporter's clothes, I was doing my little thing and interviewing everybody, but I knew this was different.

And the appointed night came. I was staying at a grubby little motel right near the project house. I remember it was the week that the Dylan album *Bringing It All Back Home* had come out and *Mr. Tambourine Man* was playing endlessly on the little Webcor hi-fi in the house. I dressed up in my tie and jacket, rented a car, and went way out away from the inner city. It was the mid-'60s flight. Dan Silverberg had grown up in Shaker Heights, but even Shaker Heights was too close now. *They* were moving into Shaker Heights. So I drove to Pepper Pike Boulevard or Parkway, way out. Some other new suburb that was just going up. And we went to his club which was plush banquettes and Mediterranean fixtures. Young investment consultants and their lovely wives and friends. I remember sitting there absolutely blanking out. Other people apparently were there, I have no recollection. And my mind was back in the project house, and that reality was so strong, and this reality so different and unpleasant and inauthentic to me. They were talking about their houses, their careers, and their kids, and I started dissimulating and there I was watching this person who used to be Andy Kopkind sitting with his old friend Dan Silverberg. And between the filet and the cheesecake with strawberries I suddenly got up and said, "Oh, I have a meeting I have to go cover."

I got in my rent-a-car and went back to the west side of inner-city Cleveland and realized that I could never do that other thing again without it being a performance of some kind. At some point later on, I integrated all these things into a sort of social matrix in which you can do something one night and do something else the next night. But the matrix at that point was exclusive. And my behavior and self-presentation started changing from that day—whom I could be comfortable with and what I was comfortable doing. I was still the journalist, but I was part of the movement too. It was the first time I was really involved.

Fergus Allen grew up in Ireland, attending Quaker schools in Dublin and Waterford. Since he graduated in civil engineering from Trinity College, Dublin, he has lived and worked in England. His first collection of poems, *The Brown Parrots of Providencia*, was published by Faber & Faber in 1993.

Ecke Bonk, a German artist, has asked us to publish in lieu of a biography the following palindrome: [AIDE MOI: O MEDIA].

William S. Burroughs, the author of *Naked Lunch, Junky, Queer, Cities of the Red Night, The Place of Dead Roads, The Western Lands,* and *The Cat Inside,* is a member of the American Academy and Institute for Arts and Letters. He lives in Lawrence, Kansas. The dream notes published here will appear in *My Education: A Book of Dreams* (Viking), to be published in 1995.

Alexander Cockburn is a syndicated columnist who contributes regularly to *The Nation, The Anderson Valley Advertiser, The Los Angeles Times,* and other newspapers. He is the author of *The Golden Age Is In Us: Journeys and Encounters, 1987–1994* (Verso). His interview with Noam Chomsky appeared in *Grand Street 50.*

Douglas Cooper's first novel, *Amnesia*, was published by Hyperion in 1994. He is collaborating with architects Diller & Scofidio on a Virtual Reality installation for the Pompidou Center in Paris, and with Peter Eisenman on a project for the Milan Triennale. *The Moron* was commissioned by Culture Lab in Toronto, as part of a colloquium on "Dipsticks: The Problem of Measurement." A version of this story will be published in a forthcoming book by Princeton Architectural Press.

Louis Faurer was born in Philadelphia in 1916. Living in New York in the late 1940s, he worked for *Harper's Bazaar, Vogue, Life,* and other magazines, and began photographing New York City street scenes. His work appeared in group shows at the Museum of Modern Art in 1948, 1955, and 1978 and his first solo show was held at the Limelight Gallery in New York in 1959. Faurer has received a photography fellowship from the National Endowment for the Arts and a Guggenheim Fellowship. He lives in New York and is represented by the Light Gallery.

B. H. Friedman has written fiction, biography, criticism, and plays. He worked in real estate from 1948 to 1963 and was introduced to various members of the art world by the art dealer Curt Valentin and others. His novels include *Yarborough, Whispers,* and *The Polygamist,* and his non-fiction includes biographies of Jackson Pollock and Gertrude Vanderbilt Whitney. He is currently editing his journal, tentatively titled *Turning Out the Lights.*

Guneli Gun was born in Turkey and educated at Hollins College, the Iowa Writers Workshop, and John Hopkins University. She is the author of *Book of Trances* and *On the Road to Baghdad,* and is the translator of *Night* by Bilge Karasu. She lives and works in Oberlin, Ohio.

Kirsty Gunn was born in New Zealand and educated at Victoria University and Oxford. She currently freelances for Condé Nast in London and is at work on her second novel. The story published here is adapted from her first novel, *Rain,* to be published by Atlantic Monthly Press in the spring of 1995.

James Haining is the founder of Salt Lick Press. He is working on a series of poems about multiple sclerosis. He lives and works in Portland, Oregon.

David Hammons was born in Springfield, Illinois in 1943. He began exhibiting in the early 1970s, and his work was the subject of a 1991–92 retrospective that traveled to P.S. 1 in New York, the Institute of Contemporary Art in Philadelphia, and the San Diego Museum of Contemporary Art. His work has been included in the Carnegie Museum of Art's *Carnegie International* in Pittsburgh, *Dislocations* at the Museum of Modern Art in New York, and the Spoleto Festival in Charleston, South Carolina. He lives and works in New York City and Rome, Italy.

Kazuo Ishiguro was born in 1954 in Japan. When he was five, he moved with his family to England, where he has lived ever since. His first novel, *A Pale View of the Hills,* was awarded the Royal Society of Literature Prize; his second, *An Artist of the Floating World,* received the Whitbred Book of the Year Award in 1986; and his third, *The Remains of the Day,* won the 1989 Booker Prize. A new novel, *The Unconsoled,* is forthcoming from Faber & Faber.

Darius H. James is the author of *Negrophobia* and *That's Blaxploitation!!!*

(to be published by St. Martin's Press in 1995), from which *Panther* is excerpted. He has written for *Spin, Penthouse,* and *Puritan.* He lives in Brooklyn, New York.

August Kleinzahler is the author of *Storm Over Hackensack, Earthquake Weather* (Moyer Bell), and a new collection of poems, *Red Sauce, Whiskey and Snow,* forthcoming from Farrar, Straus & Giroux in the spring of 1995.

Andrew Kopkind was born in New Haven in 1935. He studied philosophy at Cornell University and international relations at the London School of Economics. He was a reporter for *The Washington Post* and *Time* and joined the staff of *The New Republic* in 1964. He was, at the same time, American correspondent for *The New Statesman* in London. His reportage and analysis in the 1960s introduced the New Left to a wider public in such publications as *The New Republic, The New York Times Magazine,* and *The New York Review of Books.* In the 1970s, he wrote for *Hard Times* (which he cofounded with James Ridgeway), *Ramparts,* and *The Village Voice,* while covering the gay liberation movement and conducting *Lavender Hour* (WBCN in Boston), the first gay and lesbian radio program on American commercial radio. For the past decade he covered the cultural and political scene in America and abroad for *The Nation,* and was an invaluable presence in his role as a contributing editor to *Grand Street. The Thirty Years' War,* a collection of his work since 1965, will be published by Verso in the spring of 1995. He died in New York in October of 1994. The article that appears here is excerpted from a forthcoming book by Jean Stein.

Louise Lawler was born in Bronxville, New York in 1947. Her work was included in the 1991 *Biennial* at The Whitney Museum of American Art, the *Carnegie International* in Pittsburgh, and *Radical Scavenger(s)* at the Museum of Contemporary Art in Chicago. Recent one-person exhibitions include those at the Centre d'Art Contemporain in Geneva, Switzerland and the Monika Spruth Gallery in Cologne, Germany. Lawler lives and works in New York City where she is represented by Metro Pictures Gallery.

Sue Lenier has published two collections of poetry, *Swansongs* and *Rain Following* (Oleander Press, Cambridge). Her plays have been performed at the Edinburgh Festival Fringe and on B.B.C. Radio. She lives in East Sussex, England.

Paul St. John Mackintosh and **Maki Sugiyama** have previously translated the poems of Nakahara Chuya, a Japanese poet, to great acclaim.

Michael Moore is a native of Flint, Michigan and the producer/director of the 1989 documentary *Roger and Me*, a political satire documenting his quest to show General Motors chairman Roger B. Smith the devastion wrought by plant shutdowns in Flint. Most recently, he developed, produced, and directed the NBC series *TV Nation*.

Hilda Morley is the author of several books of poetry, most recently *Between the Rocks*, published in a limited, fine-press edition by Tangram Press. She has received Guggenheim, New York State Foundation for the Arts, and other grants. Her book *To Hold in My Hand* received the first Capricorn Award. She is currently working on a new volume of poems and a biographical memoir of her late husband, the composer Stefan Wolpe.

Margaret Morton, a documentary photographer who lives in New York City, is associate professor of art at the Cooper Union School of Art. Since 1989, she has photographed the dwellings that homeless individuals create for themselves along and underneath the streets of New York City. A selection of these photographs, *Transitory Gardens, Uprooted Lives* (Yale University Press), coauthored with Diana Balmori, was published in 1993. Her forthcoming books *The Tunnel* and *The Architecture of Despair* will be published by Yale in 1995 and 1996 respectively.

Kenzaburo Oe was born on the Japanese island of Shikoku in 1935. His novels include *The Silent Cry*, *A Personal Matter*, *Teach Us to Outgrow Our Madness*, and the forthcoming *Nip the Buds, Shoot the Kids* (Marion Boyars, New York) from which the passage published here is excerpted. His stories *The Way of Eating Fried Sausage* and *A Map of the World* (an excerpt from his novel *M/T et l'histoire des merveilles de la forêt*) have appeared in issues 38 and 43 of *Grand Street*. He was awarded the 1994 Nobel Prize for Literature.

Orhan Pamuk is the author of *The White Castle*. He lives with his wife and daughter in Istanbul. His novel *The Black Book*, from which the story here is adapted, will be published by Farrar, Straus & Giroux in 1995.

Richard Prince was born in the former Panama Canal Zone in 1949. Recent museum surveys of his work include those at the Whitney Museum of American Art, New York, the San Francisco Museum of Modern Art, the Museum Boymans-van Beuningen, Rotterdam, and the Kunstverein and Kunsthalle, Dusseldorf, Germany. He lives and works in New York where he is represented by the Barbara Gladstone Gallery.

Amy Scattergood is a graduate of Bowdoin College, Yale Divinity School, and the Iowa Writers Workshop. Her poetry has appeared in *New England Review, Indiana Review*, and *The Denver Quarterly*. She lives in Los Angeles.

Charles Simic is the author of seventeen collections of poetry, four books of prose, and numerous books of translations. He has won many awards, including a MacArthur Fellowship and a Pulitzer Prize. His new book of poems is *Wedding in Hell* (Harcourt Brace).

William T. Vollmann lived in New York from 1988 to 1990. He has just completed a manual for writers called *Wordcraft*. The stories printed here are taken from his forthcoming collection *The Atlas*. He lives and works in Sacramento, California.

Terry Williams teaches at the New School for Social Research in New York City. He is founder of the Harlem Writers Crew, an alternative writing and multimedia approach to youth education. He is currently completing a book on tunnel residents and other subterranean populations.

Fiona Wilson's poetry has appeared in various journals in the United States and the United Kingdom, most recently in *Verse, Oxford Poetry*, and forthcoming in *Pequod*. She lives in New York.

In *Grand Street 50*, the photographer Tom Powel's name was inadvertently omitted from the title page of the portfolio *The Prior Art*. In *The Society of Models* in *Grand Street 50*, the Hit Factory's name was accidentally misspelled.

PARANOIA IS
A FORM

OF AWARENESS
THIS PUBLIC SERVICE MESSAGE IS BROUGHT TO YOU BY DISASSOCIATE

ILLUSTRATIONS

ILLUSTRATIONS

The credits for the works by Henri Matisse published on pages 78, 84, and 88 of *Grand Street* 50 were given in incomplete form. All three images should have been listed as © 1994 Succession H. Matisse/ ARS New York.

The Georgia Review

——————— *Fall 1994* ———————

- *Some of Us Do It Anyway: An Interview with Harry Crews*
  by Tammy Lytal & Richard R. Russell

- Lionel Basney's *The Space for Grief*

- David Bosworth's *Killing the Covenant: The Savage Idolatry of the New World Order*

- Sanford Pinsker's *Imagining the Postmodern Family*

- Gerald Weales's *American Theater Watch, 1993-1994*

FICTION by Kirsten Backstrom, Larry Baker, & Justin Evans

POETRY by Coleman Barks, Stephen Dobyns, Rita Dove, Caroline Finkelstein, Elton Glaser, Daniel Hoffman, Kay Ryan, Charles Simic, Phillip Sterling, Jerry W. Ward Jr., & Robert Wrigley

ARTWORK: Jill Cannady's *Companions, Colleagues, & Confidants*

BOOK REVIEWS by Jeanne Braham, Judith Kitchen, Tod Marshall, Horace Montgomery, Collie Owens, & Patricia Meyer Spacks

---

249

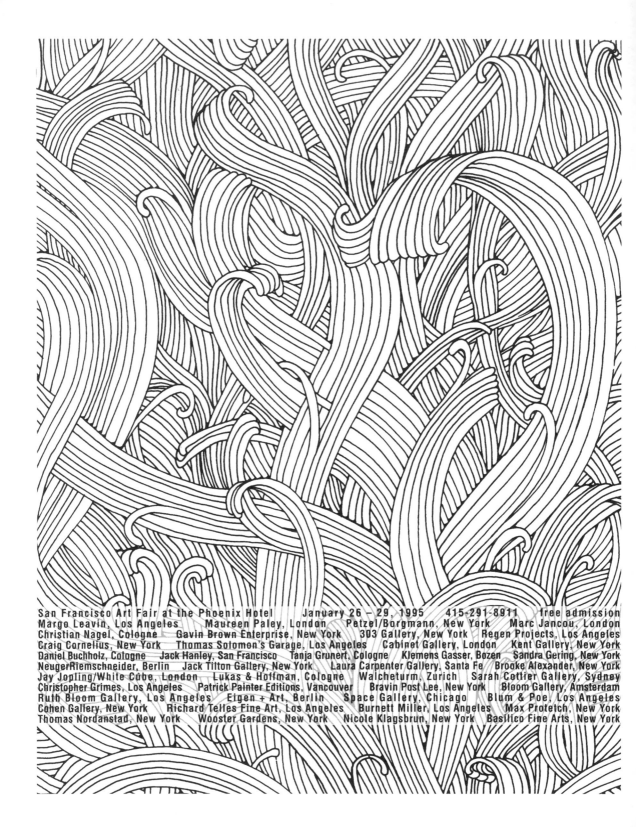

San Francisco Art Fair at the Phoenix Hotel   January 26 – 29, 1995   415-291-8911   free admission
Margo Leavin, Los Angeles   Maureen Paley, London   Petzel/Borgmann, New York   Marc Jancou, London
Christian Nagel, Cologne   Gavin Brown Enterprise, New York   303 Gallery, New York   Regen Projects, Los Angeles
Craig Cornelius, New York   Thomas Solomon's Garage, Los Angeles   Cabinet Gallery, London   Kent Gallery, New York
Daniel Buchholz, Cologne   Jack Hanley, San Francisco   Tanja Grunert, Cologne   Klemens Gasser, Bozen   Sandra Gering, New York
NeugerRiemschneider, Berlin   Jack Tilton Gallery, New York   Laura Carpenter Gallery, Santa Fe   Brooke Alexander, New York
Jay Jopling/White Cube, London   Lukas & Hoffman, Cologne   Walcheturm, Zurich   Sarah Cottier Gallery, Sydney
Christopher Grimes, Los Angeles   Patrick Painter Editions, Vancouver   Bravin Post Lee, New York   Bloom Gallery, Amsterdam
Ruth Bloom Gallery, Los Angeles   Eigen + Art, Berlin   Space Gallery, Chicago   Blum & Poe, Los Angeles
Cohen Gallery, New York   Richard Telles Fine Art, Los Angeles   Burnett Miller, Los Angeles   Max Protetch, New York
Thomas Nordanstad, New York   Wooster Gardens, New York   Nicole Klagsbrun, New York   Basilico Fine Arts, New York

THE WORLD

Issue 49

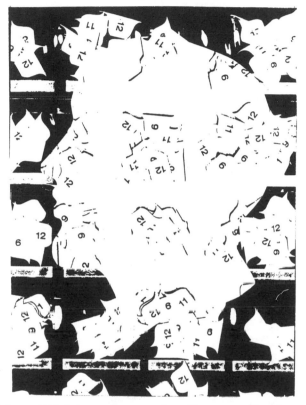

New Writing from the Poetry Project

John Godfrey, Diane Ward, Kathy Price, Jeremy Reed, Sarah Covington,
Barbara Guest, Jim Brodey, Clark Coolidge, Tom Raworth, Kathleen Large,
Amy Gerstler, Richard Foreman, Elizabeth Castagna, Larry Fagin,
Ed Friedman, Ted Greenwald, Merry Fortune, Shelia E. Murphy,
Nina Zivancevic, Alice Notley, Barbara Barg, Laurie Price,
Tom Savage, Richard Hell, Gillian McCain, Robert Hershon, Larry Zirlin,
Robert V. Hale, Laurie Price, Carol Szamatowicz, Nathanial Mackey,
Daniel & David Shapiro and Jen Hofer. Cover by Shen Chen.

$5 single issues • Subscriptions $20 for four issues

THE POETRY PROJECT
St. Mark's Church • 131 E 10 St • New York, NY 10003

ARNO SCHMIDT

COLLECTED NOVELLAS

Collected Early Fiction 1949-1964, volume 1
Translated by John E. Woods

the first in a 4-volume edition of the early works of Arno Schmidt

"An enormously important talent in the fictional line of cruel comedy that runs from Rabelais through Swift and Joyce."

—*New York Review of Books*

at better bookstores everywhere
or available directly from the publisher:
Dalkey Archive Press
Campus Box 4241, Normal, IL 61790-4241
phone orders: (309) 438-7555
($22.95 plus $1.50 p&h)
ISBN 1-56478-066-X, 440 pp.

Vol 1 No. 3 1994 $6

Cultural Permissions

Contributors:

Kirby Gookin, Thelma Golden, Jim Lewis, Laura Trippi
Douglas Blau, Ronald Jones (with Rirkrit Tiravanija, Laura Stein
Gavin Brown, Jan Avgikos, Brian Tolle, Michael Joaquin Grey
and Paul Myoda), Bob Nickas, Geno Rodriguez, Isabelle Graw
John Zinsser, Michael Corris, David Pagel, Sidney Tillim
Franklin Sirmins, Jutta Koether, Kinshasha Holman Conwill
Vasif Kortun, Olivier Zahm, Peter Fend, Sabine Vogel
Paul Myoda, Joshua Decter, John Miller, Lois Nesbitt
Howard Halle, Stephan Dillemuth, Mira Schor and Susan Bee
G. Roger Denson, Benjamin Weil, Marius Babias
David Reisman, Dennis Balk, Barbara and Howard Morse

Editor and Publisher: Joshua Decter
Senior Editor: John Miller

For subscriptions and information: Acme Journal
P.O. Box 1015
Canal Street Station
New York, N Y 10013
phone/fax: (212) 255-4422

Back Issues of Grand Street

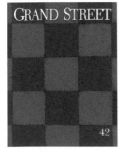

An Indispensable Collection

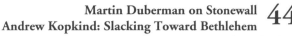
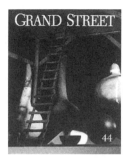

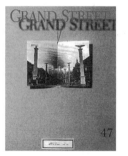

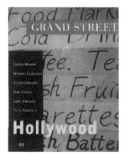
Now Available–Order While They Last

CALL 1-800-807-6548 or send name, address, issue number(s), and quantity. American Express, Mastercard, and Visa accepted; please send credit card number and expiration date. Back issues are $12.00 each ($15.00 overseas and Canada), which including postage and handling, payable in U.S. dollars.
Address orders to *Grand Street* Back Issues, 131 Varick Street, Suite 906, New York, N.Y. 10013.

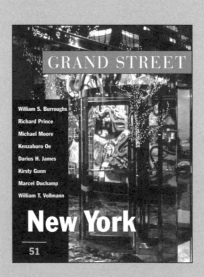